WALL, WATER AND WOODLAND GARDENS

INCLUDING THE ROCK GARDEN
AND THE HEATH GARDEN

BY

GERTRUDE JEKYLL

With a Chapter on the Asiatic Primulas

BY

G. C. TAYLOR

EIGHTH EDITION REVISED

ANTIQUE COLLECTORS' CLUB

© 1982 The Estate of Gertrude Jekyll
ISBN 0 907462 26 X
Reprinted 1986

First published 1901. This edition reprinted from the eighth
edition revised, published by Country Life, 1933, with 16
colour illustrations added 1982.

Published for the Antique Collectors' Club by the Antique
Collectors' Club Ltd.

British Library CIP Data
Jekyll, Gertrude
Wall, water and woodland gardens.—8th ed.
1. Rock gardens   2. Water gardens
3. Ornamental trees   4. Landscape gardening
I. Title
712'.6   SB454

Printed in England by the Antique Collectors' Club Ltd., Woodbridge, Suffolk

PREFACE

THERE is scarcely an English country home where some kind of gardening is not practised, while in a very large number of country places their owners have in some degree become aware of the happiness that comes of a love of flowers, and of how much that happiness increases when personal labour and study work together to a better knowledge of their wants and ways.

In this book a portion only of the great subject of horticulture is considered, namely, simple ways of using some of the many beautiful mountain plants, and the plants of marsh and water. It is intended as a guide to amateurs, being written by one of their number, who has tried to work out some of the problems presented by the use of these classes of plants to the bettering of our gardens and outer grounds.

The book does not attempt to exhaust the subject, neither does it presume to lay down the law. It is enough, in the case of the rock and wall plants, for instance, to name some of the best and easiest to grow. Those who will make such use of it as to work out any of the examples it suggests, will then have learnt so much for themselves that they will be able to profit by more learned books and more copious lists of flowers.

The large quantity of pictorial illustration is in itself helpful teaching. "I like a book with pictures" is not only an idle speech of those who open a book in order to enjoy the trivial intellectual tickling of the thing actually represented; but the illustrations are of distinct educational value, in that they present aspects of things beautiful, or of matters desirable for practice, much more vividly than can be done by the unpictured text.

I am indebted to the proprietors of *Country Life* for the use of some of the illustrations, and for a valuable list of plants and other particulars communicated to old numbers of *The Garden* by Mr. Correvon of Geneva; also to the proprietors of *Country Life* for a still larger number of subjects for illustration; to the late Sir Frank Crisp for a number of photographs of his wonderful rock-garden; and to Mr. W. Robinson for two photographs of unusual interest. I have also to acknowledge the kind help of Mr. James Hudson, who compiled the list of Water-Lilies at the end of Chapter XX.

In some cases I have made critical observations

on pictures showing portions of various English
gardens. If any apology is due to the owners of
these gardens I freely offer it, though I venture to
feel sure that they will perceive my intention to be
not so much criticism of the place itself as the suggestion of alternatives of treatment such as might
also be desirable in places presenting analogous
conditions.

G. J.

PREFACE TO EIGHTH EDITION

WITH the publication of the eighth edition of this book, the opportunity has been taken to widen its scope and bring the information up to date and into line with modern tendencies in Gardening, and so to continue to make it serve its original aim as a useful and practical handbook on modern gardening, by the inclusion of chapters on Woodland Gardening and on the Asiatic Primulas. No one did more than Miss Jekyll to turn the attention of all gardeners to the possibilities of gardening in woodland, and thirty years of horticultural discovery and the need for more natural methods of gardening have only served to bring home the wisdom and truth of her stimulating teaching, which is clearly set forth in her own precise and clear style in the chapter on the woodland garden, which she completed and passed for press only a few weeks before her death. The chapter which has been included on the Asiatic Primulas reflects the increasing interest which is being taken in this handsome race of hardy plants that are so invaluable for their colour and floral display by the waterside and in the woodland. It presents an exhaustive survey of all the best species for garden decoration, including all the more recent introductions of the last ten years, and it is hoped that it will serve as a useful and informative guide to all gardeners interested in the Primula family.

CONTENTS

CONTENTS

WALL AND WATER GARDENS

CHAPTER I

THE DRY-WALLED TERRACE GARDEN

MANY a garden has to be made on a hillside more or
less steep. The conditions of such a site naturally
suggest some form of terracing, and in connection
with a house of modest size and kind, nothing is
prettier or pleasanter than all the various ways of
terraced treatment that may be practised with the help
of dry-walling, that is to say, rough wall-building
without mortar, especially where a suitable kind of
stone can be had locally.

It is well in sharply-sloping ground to keep the
paths as nearly level as may be, whether they are in
straight lines or whether they curve in following the
natural contour of the ground. Many more beautiful
garden-pictures may be made by variety in planting
even quite straightly terraced spaces than at first
appears possible, and the frequent flights of steps,
always beautiful if easy and well proportioned, will be
of the greatest value. When steps are built in this
kind of rough terracing the almost invariable fault is
that they are made too steep and too narrow in the

tread. It is a good rule to make the steps so easy that one can run up and down, whether they are of skilled workmanship, as in the present illustration, or rough, as in that on p. 42. There is no reason or excuse for the steep, ugly, and even dangerous steps one so often sees. Unless the paths come too close together on the upper and lower terraces, space for the more easy gradient can be cut away above, and the steps can also be carried out free below; the ground cut through above being supported by dry-walling at the sides of the steps, and, where the steps stand up clear below, their sides being built up free. If for any reason this is difficult or inexpedient, a landing can be built out and the steps carried down sideways instead of up and down the face of the hill. In fact, there is no end to the pretty and interesting ways of using such walling and such groups of steps.

Where the stairway cuts through the bank and is lined on each side by the dry-walling, the whole structure becomes a garden of delightful small things. Little Ferns are planted in the joints on the shadier side as the wall goes up, and numbers of small Saxifrages and Stonecrops, Pennywort and *Erinus*, *Corydalis* and Sandwort. Then there will be hanging sheets of *Aubrietia* and Rock Pinks, *Iberis* and *Cerastium*, and many another pretty plant that will find a happy home in the cool shelter of the rocky joint. In some regions of the walling Wallflowers and Snapdragons and plants of Thrift can be established; as they ripen their seed it drifts into the openings of other joints, and the seedlings send their roots deep

EASY STEPS IN CONNEXION WITH DRY-WALLING.

into the bank and along the cool backs of the stones, and make plants of surprising health and vigour that are longer lived than the softer-grown plants in the rich flower-borders.

I doubt if there is any way in which a good quantity of plants, and of bushes of moderate size, can be so well seen and enjoyed as in one of these roughly terraced gardens, for one sees them up and down and in all sorts of ways, and one has a chance of seeing many lovely flowers clear against the sky, and of perhaps catching some sweetly-scented tiny thing like *Dianthus fragrans* at exactly nose-height and eye-level, and so of enjoying its tender beauty and powerful fragrance in a way that had never before been found possible.

Then the beautiful detail of structure and marking in such plants as the silvery Saxifrages can never be so well seen as in a wall at the level of the eye or just above or below it ; and plain to see are all the pretty ways these small plants have of seating themselves on projections or nestling into hollows, or creeping over stony surface as does the Balearic Sandwort, or standing like *Erinus* with its back pressed to the wall in an attitude of soldier-like bolt-uprightness.

In place of all this easily attained prettiness how many gardens on sloping ground are disfigured by profitless and quite indefensible steep banks of mown grass ! Hardly anything can be so undesirable in a garden. Such banks are unbeautiful, troublesome to mow, and wasteful of spaces that might be full of interest. If there must be a sloping space, and if for

"In connection with a house of modest size and kind, nothing is prettier or pleasanter than all the various ways of terraced treatment that may be practised with the help of dry-walling, that is to say, rough wall-building. . .especially where a suitable kind of stone can be had locally. [One of the great advantages] to be gained by the use of the terrace walls. . . is the display of the many shrubs as well as plants that will hang over and throw their flowering sprays all over the face of the wall. In arranging such gardens, I like to have only a very narrow border at the foot of each wall, to accommodate. . .any plant that is thankful for warmth or shelter."

any reason there cannot be a dry wall, it is better to plant the slope with low bushy or rambling things; with creeping Cotoneaster or Japan Honeysuckle, with Ivies, or with such bushes as Savin, *Pyrus japonica*, Cistus, or Berberis ; or if it is on a large scale, with the free-growing rambling Roses and double-flowered Brambles. I name these things in preference to the rather over-done Periwinkle and St. John's-wort, because Periwinkle is troublesome to weed, and soon grows into undesirably tight masses, and the *Hypericum*, though sometimes of good effect, is extremely monotonous in large masses by itself, and is so ground-greedy that it allows of no companionship.

There is another great advantage to be gained by the use of the terrace walls ; this is the display of the many shrubs as well as plants that will hang over and throw their flowering sprays all over the face of the wall.

In arranging such gardens, I like to have only a very narrow border at the foot of each wall, to accommodate such plants as the dwarf Lavender shown in the illustration, or any plant that is thankful for warmth or shelter.

In many cases, or even most, it will be best to have no border at all, but to make a slight preparation at the wall foot not apparently distinguishable from the path itself, and to have only an occasional plant or group or tuft of Fern. Seeds will fall to this point, and the trailing and sheeting plants will clothe the wall foot and path edge, and the whole thing will look much better than if it had a stiffly edged border.

I suppose the whole width of the terrace to be four-

ROUGH-HEWN STEPS LEADING FROM TERRACE TO TERRACE.

DWARF LAVENDER AT THE FOOT OF THE DRY-WALL.

teen feet. I would have the path six feet wide, allowing an extra foot for the rooting of plants next the
wall; then there would be a seven-foot width for the
border, planted with bushy things towards its outer
edge, which will be the top of the wall of the next
terrace below. These would be mostly bushes of
moderate growth, such as Lavender, Rosemary, Berberis, and *Pyrus japonica*, with the plants suitable for
partly hanging over the face of the wall. Among these
would be *Forsythia suspensa*, *Phlomis fruticosa* (Jeru-
salem Sage), and the common Barberry, so beautiful
with its coral-like masses of fruit in October, its half-
weeping habit of growth, and its way of disposing its
branches in pictorial masses. There would also be *Desmodium penduliflorum*, and above all the many kinds of
Roses that grow and flower so kindly in such a position. No one can know till they try how well many
sorts of Roses will tumble over walls and flower in
profusion. *Rosa lucida* and Scotch Briers come over
a wall nearly five feet high, and flower within a foot
from the ground; *Rosa wichuraiana* hangs over in a
curtain of delicate white bloom and polished leafage.
There is a neat and pretty evergreen form of *R. sempervirens* from Southern Italy, in leaf and habit not
unlike *wichuraiana*, but always more shy of flower,
which hangs over in masses, and in warm exposures
flowers more freely than on the flat. If one had to
clothe the face of a wall twelve feet high with hanging
wreathes of flowering Roses, there is a garden form
of *R. arvensis* that, planted at the top, will climb and
scramble either up or down, and will ramble through

other bushes to almost any extent. I know it as the Kitchen Rose, because the oldest plant I have rambles over and through some *Arbor-vitæ* just opposite the kitchen window of a little cottage that I lived in for two years. When it is in flower the mass of white bloom throws a distinctly appreciable light into the kitchen. The Ayrshire Roses are delightful things for this kind of use.

Where in steep ground the terraces come near together the scheme may comprise some heroic doings with plants of monumental aspect, for at the outer edge of one of the wall tops there may be a great group of *Yucca gloriosa* or *Y. recurva*, some of it actually planted in the wall within a course or two of the top, or some top stones may be left out; or the Yuccas may be planted as the wall goes up, with small kinds such as *Y. flaccida* a little lower down. Another such group, of different shape but clearly in relation to it, may be in the next terrace above or below. When the Yuccas are in flower and are seen from below, complete in their splendid dignity of solid leaf and immense spire of ivory bloom, against the often cloudless blue of our summer skies, their owner will rejoice in possessing a picture of perhaps the highest degree of nobility of plant form that may be seen in an English garden.

The garden of dry-walled terraces will necessarily be differently treated if its exposure is to the full southern or south-western sunshine, or to the north or north-east. In the case of the hot, dry, sunny aspect, a large proportion of the South European

AN OLD GARDEN ROSE AND HYBRID ROCK PINKS IN THE DRY-WALL.

ACHILLEA UMBELLATA NINE MONTHS AFTER PLANTING.

plants that are hardy in England and like warm places in our gardens, can be used. Many of these have greyish foliage, and it would be greatly to the advantage of the planting, from the pictorial point of view, to keep them rather near together. It should also be noted that a large proportion of them, of shrubby and half-shrubby character, are good winter plants, such as Lavender, Rosemary, *Phlomis*, *Othonnopsis*, and *Santolina*; the last, as may be seen in the illustration on p. 59, being specially well clothed in the winter months. They can be as well planted at the top edge of the wall, at the bottom, or in the face. With these plants well grouped, and the addition of some common white Pinks, and the useful hybrids of Rock Pinks; with a few grey-leaved Alpines such as *Cerastium*, *Artemisia nana*, *A. sericea*, the encrusted Saxifrages, and *Achillea umbellata*, a piece of the best possible wall-gardening can be done that will be as complete and well furnished in winter (but for the bloom of the plants) as it is in summer. *Achillea umbellata* is a plant of extreme value in wall-planting in all aspects It grows fairly fast, and from a few pieces of a pulled-apart plant will in a short time give the result shown in the illustrations; it should be replanted every three years. There is no need in such a case to remember the exact date of planting. The plant is at its best in its first and second year; then it begins to look a little straggly and over-worn. This may be taken as the signal for replanting, as in all such cases with any other plants.

Such a choice of plants would serve for quite

a long section of wall. The character of the planting might then change and gradually give way to another grouping that might be mainly of Cistuses. With these, and in the hottest wall-spaces, might come some of the South European Campanulas; *C. iso-phylla*, both blue and white, *C. garganica*, *C. fragilis*, and *C. muralis*. These gems of their kind live and do well in upright walling, whereas they would perish on the more open rockery, or could only be kept alive by some unbeautiful device for a winter protection.

Not only does the wall afford the shelter needed for plants that would otherwise be scarcely hardy, but the fact of planting them with the roots spread horizontally, and the crown of the plant therefore more or less upright instead of flat, obviates the danger that besets so many tender plants, of an accumulation of wet settling in the crown, then freezing and causing the plant to decay.

In many places where these rather tender southern plants are grown, they require a covering of sheets of glass in the winter, whereas in the wall they are safe and have no need of these unsightly contrivances.

SOME OF THE PLANTS AND SHRUBS FOR DRY-WALLED TERRACES

IN A COOL PLACE

Saxifrages, Mossy.	*Corydalis.*
Wall Pennywort.	*Erinus alpinus* (cool or warm).
Arenaria balearica.	Small Ferns.

*ACHILLEA UMBELLATA IN MID-WINTER, SIXTEEN MONTHS
AFTER PLANTING.*

(Half of the same group that is shown on p. 26 scale rather larger.)

ARABIS IN A DRY-WALL.

To Hang Down

Rock Pinks.
Iberis.
Alyssum.
Othonnopsis.

Aubrietia.
Cerastium.
Mossy Saxifrage (cool).
Arabis and double var.

In Sun or Shade

Wallflowers.
Snapdragons.
Centranthus.

Thrift.
Dianthus fragrans.

Shrubs to Hang Over from the Top

Cistus cyprius.
C. laurifolius.
Lavender.
Othonnopsis cheirifolia.
Desmodium penduliflorum.
Rosa lucida.
R. sempervirens, vars.
Euphorbia Wulfenii.

Phlomis fruticosa.
Santolina chamæcyparissus.
Rosemary.
Berberis vulgaris.
Pyrus japonica.
Rosa wichuraiana.
R. arvensis, garden vars.
Euphorbia characias.

Grey-leaved Alpine Plants for the Wall

Cerastium tomentosum.
Artemisia nana.
Stachys lanata.

Achillea umbellata.
Artemisia sericea.
Nepeta Mussini.

Plants for Hottest Places

Campanula isophylla.
C. fragilis.
Yucca gloriosa.
Y. flaccida.
Stonecrops.

Campanula garganica.
C. muralis.
Yucca recurva.
Opuntia, in var.

CHAPTER II

A ROCK-GARDEN may be anything between an upright wall and a nearly dead level. It is generally an artificial structure of earth and stones, and alas! only too often it is an aggregation of shapeless mounds and hollows made anyhow. Such a place is not only ugly but is very likely not suitable for the plants that are intended to grow in it. If any success in the cultivation of rock-plants is expected, it is only reasonable to suppose that one must take the trouble to learn something about the plants, their kinds and their needs, and it is equally necessary to take the trouble to learn how their places are to be prepared. Happily for the chances of success and pleasure in this delightful kind of gardening the right way is also the most beautiful way. There is no need to surround every little plant with a kind of enclosure of stones, set on edge and pointing to all four points of the compass; it is far better to set the stones more or less in courses or in lines of stratification, just as we see them in nature in a stone quarry or any mountain side where surface denudation has left them standing out clear in nearly parallel lines. It matters not the least whether the courses are far apart or

SNAPDRAGONS CLOTHING A DRY-WALL.

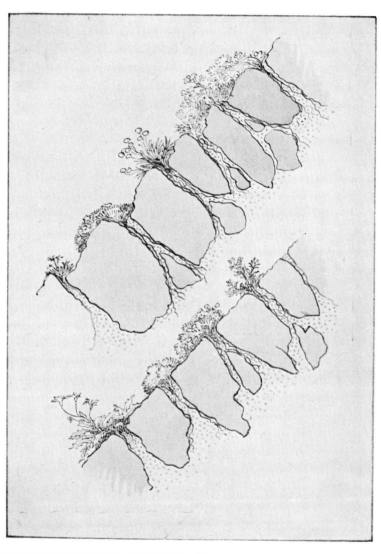

DIAGRAM (SECTION) *SHOWING* ALTERNATIVE ARRANGEMENT
OF THE FACE OF THE STONES *IN A ROCK-WALL
AT AN ANGLE OF* 45°.

near together; this is naturally settled by the steepness of the ground. In a wall they are necessarily close, and in very steep ground it is convenient to build them with the courses rather near each other. In such a case as a steep slope with an angle of 45 degrees, the face of the rock-bank could be built in either of the two ways shown in the diagram. Both will suit the plants. The flatter the angle of the ground the further apart may be the rocky courses, as the danger of the earth washing away is diminished. If the stone is not in large pieces, it will be found a good plan in rather steep banks to begin at the path level with a few courses of dry-walling, and then to make an earthy shelf and then another rise of two or three courses of walling, using the two or three courses to represent one thickness of deeper stone. But in any case the rock-builder should make up his mind how the courses should run and keep to the same rule throughout, whether the stones lie level or dip a little to right or left as they generally do in nature. But whether a stone lies level or not as to the right and left of its front face, it should always be laid so that its back end tips down into the ground, and its front face, when seen in profile, looks a little upward.

This, it will be seen, carries the rain into the ground instead of shooting it off as it would do if it were laid the other way, like the tile or slate on a building.

As for the general shape or plan of the rock-garden, it must be governed by the nature of the ground and the means and material at disposal. But whether it will be beautiful or not as a structure must depend on the knowledge and good taste of the person who plans it and sees it carried out.

As mentioned elsewhere, it is both highly desirable and extremely convenient to have different sections of the garden for the plants from different geological formations, therefore we will suppose that a portion is of limestone, and another of granite, and a third of sandstone with peat. If this sandstone and peat is mainly in the shadiest and coolest place, and can have a damp portion of a few square yards at its foot, it will be all the better. Of course if a pool can be managed, or the rock-garden can be on one or both banks of a little stream or rill, the possibilities of beautiful gardening will be endless.

In making the dry-walling the stones should all tip a little downwards at the back, and the whole face of the wall should incline slightly backward, so that no drop of rain is lost, but all runs into the joints. Any loose earth at the back of the stones must be closely rammed. If this is done there is no danger of the wall bursting outward and coming down when there is heavy rain. Any space backward of newly moved earth behind the wall must also be rammed and made firm in the same way.

The two illustrations of a bit of dry wall freshly put up give an idea of the way it is built. The one containing the angle shows how the stones are tipped back, while the one with the straight front shows how spaces at some of the joints and between the courses are left for planting. If the scheme of planting is

DRY ROCK-WALLING, SHOWING HOW THE STONES TIP BACK.

DRY ROCK-WALLING, SHOWING HOW SPACES ARE LEFT BETWEEN THE STONES.

matured and everything at hand as the wall goes up,
it is much best to plant as the stones are laid.   The
roots can then be laid well out, and larger plants can
be used than if they were to be put in when the wall
is completed.

In making the steps that go with such dry-walling
it will not be necessary that they should be entirely
paved with stones.   If the front edge is carefully fitted
and fixed the rest can be levelled up with earth and
the sides and angles planted with bits of Mossy Saxifrages or other small growths.   This is also a capital
way of making steps in steep wood paths.   In such
places the use of thick wooden slab as an edging is a
much worse expedient, for in wet or wintry weather it
becomes extremely slippery and dangerous.

The steps themselves will become flower gardens;
only the front edges need be cemented; indeed, if the
stones are large and heavy enough to be quite firm
there need be no cement; but if two or three stones
are used to form the edge of a four-foot-wide step it is
just as well to make a cement joint to fix the whole
firmly together.   This fixing need not be made to
show as a conspicuous artificial joint; it can be kept
well down between the stones, and spaces left above
and below to form many a little nook where a tiny
Fern may be planted, or a little tuft of some other
small plant—any plant that one may most wish to see
there.   If the space is cool and shady the little
Saxifraga Cymbalaria is a charming thing.   It is an
annual, but always grows again self-sown; in the
depth of winter its cheerful tufts of little bluntly-lobed

leaves look fresh and pretty in the joints of stones.   It flowers quite early in the year and then withers away completely, but the seeds sow themselves, and so without any one taking thought or trouble it renews itself faithfully from year to year.   Many small Ferns will also be quite happy in the front joints of the shady steps, such as *Cheilanthes vestita, Cystopteris fragilis* and *C. dickieana, Asplenium Trichomanes, A. Ruta-muraria, Ceterach,* and the Woodsias.

The little creeping *Arenaria balearica* will grow up the cool side of the wall or the front edge of steps and be a carpet of vivid green in deepest winter, and in June will show a galaxy of little white stars on inch-long thread-like stalks that shiver in the prettiest way to the puffing of a breath of wind or the weight of raindrops of a summer shower.

In a couple of years or even less, small Mosses will appear on the stones themselves, and the spores of Ferns wind-blown will settle in the stony face and in the joints ; then will come the delight of seeing these lovely things growing spontaneously, and coming willingly to live in the homes we have made ready for them.

No little flowering plant seems more willing to take to such a place than *Erinus alpinus.*   As soon as steps grow mossy (even if they are of solid bricklayer's work with mortar joints), if a few seeds of *Erinus* are sown in the mossy tufts they will gladly grow as shown in the illustration (p. 45), where this cheerful plant has been established on some solid steps of rough sand-stone leading to a loft, and now scatters its own seed

ROUGH STEPS BETWEEN DRY-WALLED TERRACES.

STEPS IN A ROUGH GRASS BANK : STONES CEMENTED AT FRONT.

and is quite at home as a well-settled colony making natural increase. This is an extreme case, for the little Alpine has nothing whatever to grow in but the mossy tufts that have gathered of themselves within the time, some eight years, since the steps were built.   Had the steps been of dry-walling, such as was described in the early part of the chapter, they would have grown all the quicker, having the more favourable conditions of a better root-run.

CHAPTER III

THE ROCK-WALL IN SUN

MANY of the most easily grown Alpines are just as happy in a sunny wall as in the shade. So beneficial to the root is contact with the cool stone, that plants that would perish from drought in the lighter soils and fierce sun-heat of our southern counties remain fresh and well nourished in a rock-wall in the hottest exposure. Moreover, in walls all plants seem to be longer lived. Those of the truly saxatile plants, whose way of growth is to droop over rocks and spread out flowering sheets, are never so happy as in a rock-wall. But it cannot be too often repeated that to get good effects a few kinds only should be used at a time. So only can we enjoy the full beauty of the plant and see what it really can do for us; so only can we judge of what the plant really is, and get to know its ways. In many of those rock-plants that are grown from seed, individuals will be found to vary, not only in the colour and size of the bloom, but in other characters, so that the plant cannot be judged by one example only. Look at the variety in trees—in Birches, in Hollies, in Oaks! Still more is this natural variation noticeable in small plants that are close to the eye. In

44

ERINUS IN ROUGH STONE STEPS TO A LOFT : THE STEPS HAVE CEMENTED JOINTS.

*ALPINE PLANTS IN A SUNNY LIMESTONE WALL;
SAXIFRAGA LONGIFOLIA, ERINUS, PHYTEUMA COMO-
SUM, ETC.*

watching a number of the same kind one learns how to judge them ; one sees in Cerastium, for instance, such as one of the many tufts hanging out of the wall in the picture, that one tuft has a brighter and better appearance than the next(p. 49).Then one sees that the flower, which at first one had thought was whiter than its neighbour, is not different in colour, but has rather wider petals, and that they open more and lie a little flatter, and that the leaf is somewhat broader and its downy covering slightly heavier and therefore whiter looking.

Nothing is a better lesson in the knowledge of plants than to sit down in front of them, and handle them and look them over just as carefully as possible ; and in no way can such study be more pleasantly or conveniently carried on than by taking a light seat to the rock-wall and giving plenty of time to each kind of little plant, examining it closely and asking oneself, and it, why this and why that ? Especially if the first glance shows two tufts, one with a better appearance than the other ; not to stir from the place until one has found out why and how it is done, and all about it. Of course a friend who has already gone through it all can help on the lesson more quickly, but I doubt whether it is not best to do it all for oneself.

Then the hanging plants, *Cerastium, Alyssum, Aubrietia, Silene, Arabis, Gypsophila, Saponaria,* Rock Pinks and the like, though they grow quite happily on the level, do not show their true habit as they do when they are given the nearly upright wall out of which they can hang. There are plenty of plants for the

level, and this way of growing in hanging sheets
is in itself a very interesting characteristic, pointing to the use of many beautiful things in circumstances that could not otherwise be dealt with so
satisfactorily.

The Rock Pinks and their hybrids are very important wall-plants of the hanging class. The hybrids for such use are derived from *Dianthus cæsius*
(the Cheddar Pink), *D. plumarius*, *D. superbus*, *D.
fragrans*, and possibly others. *D. fragrans* and its
double variety are delightful wall-plants; the double
is that wonderful tiny white Pink whose scent is
like the quintessence of that of Jasmine; a scent
almost too powerful. Seed of these hybrids can be
had by the name of Hybrid Rock Pinks; it is easily
grown and yields interesting varieties, all capital
wall and rock plants.

The Rock Pinks are equally happy in a wall in
sun or shade; but as we are just now considering
the plants that will bear the hottest places, among
the most important, and at the same time the most
beautiful, will be some of the tender Campanulas
of Southern Italy, and others that are usually found
tender or difficult of culture in England. *Campanula
garganica*, a native of rocks and walls in that curious
promontory of Gargano that stands out into the
Adriatic (the spur on the heel of Italy), is often an
uncertain plant in our gardens. But planted in a
cleft in very steep, almost wall-like rock-work, or
still better in an actual wall in the hottest exposure,
where it cannot suffer from the moisture that is

CERASTIUM IN THE SUNNY ROCK-WALL.

CAMPANULA GARGANICA IN SUNNY ROCK-WORK.

so commonly fatal to it, it will thrive and flower abundantly.

This species, with other Campanulas that are absolutely saxatile, should in England always be grown in a wall or perpendicular rock-work. The same treatment suits *C. Raineri*, the yellow-flowered *C. petræa* of the Tyrol, and Campanulas *muralis, Elatine, elatinoides, excisa, macrorhiza,* and *mirabilis.* That the same plan is suitable to *C. isophylla* may be seen by the illustration showing a tuft flowering in a wall facing south-west, in a garden thirty-five miles south-west of London (p. 54).

Places should also be given to the tenderer of the Lithospermums, *L. Gastoni* and *L. graminifolium. Graminifolium* is a neat bushy-looking plant; both have the flowers of the fine blue colour that is so good a character of the genus. In hottest exposures in Devon and Cornwall and the Isle of Wight there would even be a chance of success with *L. rosmarinifolium,* the "Blue Flower" of the Island of Capri. Its colour may be said to be the loveliest blue in nature. It has not the violent intensity of the Gentian, but a quality entirely its own. If one may without exaggeration speak of a blue that gives the eye perfect happiness, it would be this most perfect blue of the lovely Gromwell of the cliffs of Capri. But it *must* have sun and air and full exposure, or the colour is wanting in quality, therefore it is not a plant for the unheated greenhouse. The easily grown *L. prostratum* likes a rather cooler place, and is more a plant for the rock-garden or for grassy banks. This most useful trailer is not particular about soil, though the Lithospermums as a genus are lime-loving things.

Another important race of plants for the hot wall are the various kinds of *Iberis*. All will do well. The commonest perennial kind, *I. sempervirens*, shows new beauties in the wall. Still better is the handsomer *I. correæfolia*, larger both of leaf and flower. In the south of England we may also have *I. gibraltarica* and *I. tenoreana*, both white, tinted with pink or lilac, and *I. Pruiti*, pure white, all South European plants. These are short-lived perennials, scarcely more than biennials, but they come well from seed which should be sown in the wall; the unmoved seedlings will do much better than any transplanted ones.

Closely allied to the Iberises and capital wall-plants, doing well in all soils, but preferring lime, are the Æthionemas, mostly small neat plants with bluish leaves and pretty pink flowers. *Æ. coridifolium* or *pulchellum*, from Asia Minor, is charming against grey stones, while the Syrian *Æ. grandiflorum* is like a beautiful little pink-flowered bush. Rabbits are very fond of this family of plants, indeed they seem to favour the *Cruciferæ* in general. When I first grew the Æthionemas, forgetting their relationship to Iberis, I put them in a place accessible to rabbits; the rabbit being the better botanist recognised them at once, much to my loss. But in the wall they are safe.

The sunny wall is also the true place for the Stone-

"In making the steps. . . it will not be necessary that they should be entirely paved with stones. If the front edge is carefully fitted and fixed the rest can be levelled up with earth and the side angles planted with bits of Mossy Saxifrages or other small growths. . . The steps themselves will become flower gardens."

CAMPANULA ISOPHYLLA IN THE ROCK-WALL IN SUN. *(Flowers one inch diameter.)*

IBERIS AND CERASTIUM IN THE DRY-WALL.

STONECROP (SEDUM SPURIUM) IN THE SUNNY ROCK-WALL.

crops large and small, from the tiny *Sedum glaucum*
and the red-tinted *S. lydium* and brittle *dasyphyllum*,
through the many good kinds of moderate size, of
which *pulchellum*, *kamtschaticum*, and *Ewersii* are important, to the large-sized *S. spectabile* blooming in
September. Among these, one of the most useful is
S. spurium in three colourings ; pink, a deeper colouring near crimson, and a dull white. It is one of the
easiest plants to grow ; a few little pieces (they
need scarcely be rooted) will quickly take hold, and
a year hence make sheets of pretty succulent growth
smothered with bloom in middle summer.

The pretty Phloxes of the *setacea* group are capital
plants in the hot wall ; in their second and third
year hanging down in sheets ; the only one that
does not hang down is the charming pink " Vivid,"
which has a more tufted habit. The free-growing
P. Stellaria, one of the same family, should not be
forgotten. Its colour, a white tinged with faint
purple, makes it suitable for accompanying Aubrietias, which do well both in sun and shade.

There is a lovely little labiate, *Stachys corsica*,
which is a delightful small plant to grow in level
joints ; it is not much known, but is desirable as a
gem for the warm wall. *Arnebia echioides* is also a
good wall-plant.

It will be important that the wall, especially if it is
of any height, should have a crown of bushy things
at its top ; and not a crown only, for some shrubby
and half-shrubby plants should come down the face
here and there to a depth of two or three joints, and

occasionally even more. The plants for this use will
be *Cistus* and *Helianthemum*, Lavender, both the large
and the dwarf kinds, Rosemary, *Phlomis*, *Santolina*
(Lavender Cotton), Southernwood, *Olearia Haastii*,
Eurybia gunniana (hardy only in the south of
England), *Cassinia fulvida*, *Berberis Aquifolium* and
B. vulgaris (the common Barberry with the beautiful coral fruits), Scotch Briers, *Rosa lucida* and *Rosa
wichuraiana*, and any other beautiful small shrubs,
preferably evergreen. Also some of the pleasantest
of the Sweet Herbs, Hyssop and Catmint (beloved
of cats), both beautiful garden plants, and Rue for
the sake of its pretty growth and blue leaves; also
Sage, especially the variety with purple leaves. These,
or rather a few of them at a time, in very carefully
selected association, would be grouped upon the top
and a little way down.

It will have a good effect, if one of these more important bush-like plants, in the case of a dry wall from
eight to ten or more feet high, swept right down with
a broken or slightly curving diagonal line from top to
bottom, with some more plants of the same on the lower
level at the wall's foot. For this use *Othonnopsis*,
Nepeta, Hyssop, dwarf Lavender, and *Santolina* would
be among the best ; *Santolina* being especially valuable,
as it is excellent in winter and never untidy at any time.

The neat little *Scabiosa Pterocephala* must have a
place. It is a good plan to have a section of the
wall devoted mainly to plants of grey foliage ; here
would be the place for this, in company with *Achillea
umbellata* and *Artemisia sericea* and others of this

LAVENDER COTTON (SANTOLINA) IN THE DRY-WALL IN MID-WINTER.

DOUBLE ARABIS.

warmth-loving genus; and in the grey part of the wall there will be Southernwood and Catmint (*Nepeta Mussini*), Hyssop and Lavender Cotton, and the curious, almost blue-leaved, *Othonnopsis cheirifolia.* Many of these will be among the plants just named, but to make this clear and easy for reference they will be put together in the list at the end of the chapter.

The hardy Fuchsias will also be good plants for the head and foot of the wall, and the pretty little *F. pumila* and *F. globosa* for the wall itself.

There are two of the small St. John's-worts that must not be forgotten, *Hypericum Coris*, a perfect gem among dwarfer shrub-like plants, and *H. repens*, its exact opposite in habit, for *H. coris* stands up erect, and *H. repens* hangs straight down like Moneywort in a window-box.

It would be tempting in Cornwall to try the Caper plant (*Capparis spinosa*) and the hardier of the Mesembryanthemums that do so well in the Scilly Islands; the best to try would be *M. blandum* in its two varieties—*album* and *roseum*, seldom entirely out of bloom; the straw-coloured *M. edule* and its handsome crimson-flowered ally, *M. rubro-cinctum; M. glaucum*, one of the hardiest and finest, with large canary-yellow flowers; and *M. deltoides*, which forms a dense curtain when it is allowed to hang, and fills the air in spring with the vanilla-like scent of its small but countless pink blossoms.

With these, and in a part of the wall specially prepared with rather larger spaces between the stones in the courses, some of the hardy Opuntias would be particularly suitable ; they are mentioned more at length in the chapters on rock-gardens. Here would also be the most suitable place for the Euphorbias.

Several of the *Edraianthus* (now better known as *Wahlenbergia*), pretty plants of the Campanula family, that are often lost in gardens from winter damp, will be safe in the sunny wall. The best will be *W. dalmatica* and *W. Pumilio*. Another branch of the *Campanulaceæ*, the Phyteumas, are of special value in the wall, and will do nowhere so well. The most usually cultivated are *P. comosum*, *P. hemisphæricum*, and *P. orbiculare*. Other pretty plants, also often lost in the usual forms of rock-garden, are *Acantholimon venustum* and *A. glumaceum ;* they are allied to Thrift.

Many of these plants are best propagated by fresh seed, which can be sown as soon as it ripens in adjoining joints and crevices. It should also be remembered that there are several annuals that can with advantage be sown in the wall ; some of the most suitable would be *Iberis odorata, Saponaria calabrica,* and *Silene pendula,* also the little blue Stonecrop (*Sedum cæruleum*).

The lovely little *Petrocallis pyrenaica* is a true plant for the sunny wall in its upper joints. The larger growth of *Stobæa purpurea* will also suit the top joints of the upper courses, or the warm place at the wall-foot. It is a thing that will not only do well in such places, but that so used will look quite at its best. To those who are unacquainted with it it may be described as a thistle-like plant with silvery-green spiny foliage

ROCK PINKS IN THE DRY-WALL.

ARABIS AND IBERIS IN THE DRY-WALL.

and leafy stems, and an abundance of pale purplish
wide-open bloom, large for the size of the plant.
Most of the Thistles, however handsome in leaf, are
disappointing in flower. This good plant, on the
contrary, surprises by the size and quality of its
bloom. It is not a plant to mix up with other
things in a border, but exactly right for the hot
rock-wall.

Parochetus communis must not be forgotten. It is
one of the flowers of perfect blue, a delight and surprise
to see on a little plant that looks like a humble Clover.
Being a native of Nepaul, it is not always hardy in
English gardens, but the shelter of the wall will preserve it in any of our southern districts.

The foot of the wall will be best if it is not planted
closely all along, but if occasionally some handsome
warmth-loving plant is there in a tuft or group. Some
of the plants most suitable for this place will be
Acanthus, *Iris stylosa*, Crinums and *Plumbago Larpentæ;* and of smaller plants, *Anomatheca cruenta,
Anemone fulgens*, and in the south, *Amaryllis Belladonna, Pancratium illyricum*, and *Zephyranthes carinata.*
An occasional bush at the wall-foot would also come
well, such as Rosemary, *Cistus lusitanicus, Veronica
hulkeana, Ozothamnus rosmarinifolius*, or *Griselinia
littoralis.*

Wonderful is the pictorial quality of Ivy, and its
power of assimilation with the forms and surfaces of
ancient buildings. For a permanent covering of anything ugly of brick or stone it is also a most helpful
auxiliary, and though I am just now considering ways

of using what are more of the nature of flowering plants, the merits of this grand climber must never be forgotten. There are often places where such a wall-garden as has been described may need some dark and quiet background. If at the end of such a scene any wall or building returned forward square with the wall, here would be the place for Ivy. Indeed there are many vast piles of building whose grim severity could endure the presence of nothing of a less serious character. Thus this great outer wall of the Alhambra, towering up in its massive simplicity, could have borne no other climbing plant than its one great sheet of Ivy.

PLANTS FOR THE SUNNY ROCK-WALL

Cerastium, Alyssum, Aubrietia, Silene, Arabis, Gypsophila, Saponaria, Dianthus hybs., D. fragans, plumarius, superbus. (These will hang down.)
Campanula garganica, Raineri, petræa, muralis, Elatine, elatinoides, excisa, macrorhiza, mirabilis, isophylla.
Lithospermum Gastoni, graminifolium.
Iberis sempervirens, correæfolia, tenoreana, gibraltarica, Pruiti.
Æthionema coridifolium, grandiflorum.
Sedum glaucum, lydium, dasyphyllum, pulchellum, kamtschaticum, spurium, Ewersii, &c.
Gnaphalium Leontopodium.

Fuchsia gracilis, Riccartoni, pumila, globosa.
Hypericum Coris, repens.
Mesembryanthemum blandum, edule, rubro-cinctum, glaucum, deltoides.
Wahlenbergia dalmatica, Pumilio.
Phyteuma comosum, hemisphæricum, orbiculare.
Acantholimon glumaceum, venustum.
Stachys corsica.
Lavender.
Santolina.
Eurybia gunniana.
Hyssopus officinalis.
Scabiosa Pterocephala.
Othonnopsis cheirifolia.
Onosma tauricum.
Primula Forrestii.

A DRY-WALL IN LATE MAY.

LAVENDER IN SUNNY DRY-WALLING.

Phlox setacea and vars., *P. Stellaria.*

Cistus, Helianthemum and vars.

Berberis Aquifolium, vulgaris.

Rosa spinosissima, lucida, wichuraiana

Olearia Haastii.

Cassinia fulvida.

Nepeta Mussini.

Artemisia sericea.

Parochetus communis.

Arnebia echioides.

Rosmarinum officinale.

Artemisia Abrotanum.

Achillea umbellata.

Petrocallis pyrenaica.

(By seed) *Iberis odorata, Saponaria calabrica, Silene pendula, Sedum cœruleum.*

At the Foot of the Wall

Acanthus.

Crinum, vars.

Anomatheca cruenta.

Amaryllis Belladonna.

Zephyranthes carinata.

Cistus lusitanicus.

Ozothamnus rosmarinifolius.

Stobæa purpurea.

Iris stylosa.

Plumbago Larpentæ.

Anemone fulgens.

Pancratium illyricum.

Rosemary.

Veronica hulkeana.

Griselinia littoralis.

CHAPTER IV

THE ROCK-WALL IN SHADE

A DRY wall with a northern or eastern exposure offers just as free a field for beautiful planting as one that looks towards the sun, and it may be assumed that quite two-thirds of the plants advised for the sunny wall will flower and do well in the cooler one also, while this will have other features distinctly its own. For whereas on the sunny side many South European species, and members of the sun-loving succulent families, will find a suitable home, the cool wall will present a series of garden-pictures almost equal in number though dissimilar in character.

What will be most conspicuous in the cool wall will be a luxuriant growth of hardy Ferns, both native and exotic ; indeed the main character of its furnishing will be cool greenery in handsome masses, though flowers will be in fair proportion. Here again, if the wall-garden is to be seen at its best, and if the plants are to be shown as well as possible, it will not do to throw together one each of a quantity of kinds, but a fair number of two or three kinds at a time should be arranged in a kind of ordered informality. No actual recipe or instructions can be given for such planting, though somewhat of the spirit of it may be appre-hended from the diagram p. 139, in which the groups

AUBRIETIA AND CERASTIUM IN A DRY-WALL AND BUTTRESS.

Of successful garden plantings Gertrude Jekyll wrote: "There will be, alike to the plant lover and to the garden artist, the satisfaction of a piece of happy gardening, without strain or affectation, beautiful and delightful in all its parts and growing easily and pleasantly out of its environment."

of each kind of plant are represented by the different ways of hatching.

It would be well to get into the way of this kind of planting as a general rule, though here and there one isolated plant of very distinct character would have a good effect.

At the foot of the wall would be grand tufts of the largest of the British Ferns, Male Fern, Lady Fern, Harts-tongue, Osmunda, and Shield Fern, and with these, handsome foreigners such as *Struthiopteris germanica* and several North American kinds. The cool pale fronds of Harts-tongue (*Scolopendrium*), in form and texture so unlike most other Ferns, are valuable not only for their own sake but for fostering the feeling of shade and coolness that is the main character of this portion of the garden. When established at the wall's foot they are of all Ferns the most willing to increase by the sowing of their own spores, though this can easily be helped by shaking a frond whose fructification is mature along some joint where a young growth of it is desirable. Be it remembered that though most Ferns love a bit of peat, Harts-tongue rejoices in a strong loam, also that *Polypodium calcareum*, as its specific name says plainly, will be thankful for lime. The little *Ruta muraria* is also a lime lover. The common Polypody is hardly ever so handsome as in a cool wall, while its relatives the Oak and Beech Ferns will be quite at home in wide joints.

If a specially cool and moist spot is noticed while the wall is building it will be well to leave out a block or two in a couple of courses, and to form a little Fern cave for the delicate Filmy Ferns (*Hymenophyllum*), and if the garden should be near the sea on our south coast there would be a chance of success with the Sea Spleenwort (*Asplenium marinum*) planted in a deep joint.

The delicately beautiful *Cystopteris,* in several kinds, will be one of the best things in the wall, also the dainty little *Woodsias.* The difficult Holly-Fern will do well in a deep horizontal wall joint, and Parsley Fern (*Allosorus*) will be contented with a cool cleft if liberally fed with chips of slate.

The wide family of Saxifrages will be largely represented in the cool rock-wall. This is a group of plants that presents so many different forms that it is one of the most puzzling to amateurs, but it is much simplified, if, putting aside some of its outlying members, one thinks of it in its relation to the wall as mainly of three kinds; the London Pride, the mossy, and the silvery or encrusted kinds. Everybody knows London Pride (*Saxifraga umbrosa*) as a pretty plant in garden edgings and for ordinary rock-garden use, but I doubt if it is ever so charming as when grown in the cool wall, when its dainty clouds of pink bloom are seen puffing out from among Fern-frond masses. Then, once seen, it is easy to recognise the Mossy Saxifrages, of which *S. hypnoides* of our northern mountains is the best known. Then no one who has once seen any examples of the silvery or encrusted Saxifrages, with their stiff, mostly strap-shaped leaves bearing along their saw-like edges that miracle of adornment of limy incrustation, could fail to recognise the others of this branch of the family. Most of them thrive in calcareous soil. They

A BRICK WALL IN THE FIRST STAGES OF PLANTING.

CAMPANULA PERSICIFOLIA AND ROCK PINKS IN A
COOL WALL.

vary in size from the tiny *S. cæsia* to the large
S. longifolia, whose huge rosette, which shows in the
illustration on p. 46, is followed by a great panicle
of creamy white flower sometimes two feet long
(see p. 223).   No plant, except perhaps *Ramondia*, is
more grateful for the upright position.

The Mossy Saxifrages may be at once recognised
by their mossy appearance.   They are for joints near
the bottom and the foot of the wall.   The close mossy
form seems to open out and stiffen as it leads to
the handsome *S. Camposi* and to *S. ceratophylla* and
others of this intermediate class.   Another section of
the Saxifrages, somewhat mossy in appearance though
not classed with them, are *S. burseriana* and *S. juni-
perina*.   They are the earliest to bloom, the flowers
opening in February ; large and pure white, in
striking contrast to the close thick tufts of dark
green foliage.   Others of the smaller Saxifrages that
will find a place in the wall are the yellow-flowered
S. sancta, not unlike the last as to its leafy tuft ;
S. oppositifolia, forming spreading or hanging sheets
with red-purple bloom ; and the double-flowered form
of the native *S. granulata*.   Collectors and careful
growers have largely increased the numbers of good
Saxifrages, especially in the encrusted and cushion
(Kabschia) kinds.   For the best kinds a good catalogue
such as that of Messrs. R. Wallace & Co. should be con-
sulted.   *S. Cymbalaria* is an annual that will always
sow itself ; the seedlings are bright and pretty through
the depth of winter.   Several of these Saxifrages, such
as *S. longifolia*, will do well on the warm wall also,
but they are better seen and enjoyed on the cool one.

In an important position in the cool wall will be a good planting of *Ramondia pyrenaica*. This excellent plant cannot be too highly esteemed. Its home in nature is in cool clefts in mountain gorges, where it constantly receives the spray of the torrent or the mountain mist. It is best in the lower part of the wall, but if the wall is of fair height and backed by a cool mass of earth, it is well to have it on the eye level. Near it should be a plant of the same family, *Haberlea rhodopensis*, smooth-leaved, and with much the same habit of growth and yet of quite different appearance.

The wall will give an opportunity for succeeding with many Alpine Primulas, some of them difficult in ordinary rock cultivation. Alpine Auriculas and any garden Primroses will be charming in some of the lower joints, and the lovely *P. Monroi*, or more properly *P. involucrata*, one of the most dainty of its family, will here do well. Others worth growing in the wall will be *P. Allionii*, *P. glutinosa*, *P. marginata*, *P. nivalis*, and *P. viscosa*.

The beautiful Androsaces, good alike in sun and shade, will have their place in the wall. The Himalayan *A. lanuginosa* seems to be one of the most willing to grow in English gardens, where its silky rosettes of foliage and pretty heads of pink flowers will fall over the face of the rocks, clothing them in a charming manner. *A. Laggeri* of the Pyrenees and *A. carnea* and *A. Chamæjasme* of the Swiss and Austrian Alps should also have a place.

Anemone apennina should be planted in the lower

EDELWEISS.

RAMONDIA PYRENAICA. (*Flowers an inch across.*)

joints and also *Anemone sylvestris,* while *A. Hepatica* is never so well pleased as when its roots are close to or among stones.

Snapdragons are grand wall-plants, both in sun and shade. I think the tender colourings, white, yellow, and pinkish, are the most suitable for the cool exposure, and the fine dark crimson reds and mixed colourings for the warm one.

The many kinds of Houseleek (*Sempervivum*) are perhaps better suited for joints in the warmer side of the wall and warm spaces in the rock-garden, though many will thrive in the cool wall.

Many a plant that one would scarcely have thought of putting in the wall will come there of its own will. Such a lesson I learnt many a year ago from the pretty little *Smilacina bifolia,* which is by nature a woodland plant. I had put some on the top of a piece of dry-walling facing north, to fill the space temporarily while some Andromedas were growing that were to crown the wall-top. The little plant grew downward into the chink as the picture shows and then spread along the next lower course, making itself quite at home (p. 83).

Two of the Acænas will be welcome, namely, *A. microphylla* and *A. pulchella.* The first is the one most commonly grown, but *A. pulchella* has merit, not only on account of the pretty form of the delicately-cut leaves, but from their unusual bronze colouring. In the wall also one can more easily escape their burrs, which are always too ready to catch hold of clothing.

Moneywort (*Lysimachia nummularia*) will be beautiful hanging down among the Ferns, and associated with *Corydalis ochroleuca*. *Waldsteinia fragarioides*, with its bright yellow bloom and brightly polished leaves, must not be forgotten.

Campanula, that large genus that yields species of the highest beauty for nearly every kind of gardening, will be represented by several ; by *C. carpatica* and *C. turbinata,* as good in shade as in sun ; by the tallest of all, *C. pyramidalis*, a grand wall-plant in the milder parts of our climate, and by the handsome *C. latifolia* (best in the white form), by *C. persicifolia,* and by some of the smaller kinds, which will include *C. pusilla* and the lovely dwarf *C. cæspitosa,* both pale blue and white. They run along the joints, throwing up their little bells in such quantities that they jostle one another and are almost overcrowded. The branch of the same family detached under the name of *Symphyandra* contains some charming flowers that thrive in such a place as the cool dry wall, *S. pendula* doing well ; here also *S. Hoffmanni* would be at home.

Arenaria balearica is described elsewhere as a capital cool wall-plant, growing up from below ; not only rooting in the joints but clothing the whole face of the stones with a kind of close skin of its tiny stalk and leaf, so that every stony hollow and projection can be clearly traced through it. *A. montana* has larger flowers and a different way of growth, but it is a good plant for the wall.

Two little plants of neat growth and small white bloom should have a place—*Hutchinsia alpina* and

SMILACINA BIFOLIA. (*One-third life size.*)

CAMPANULA PUSILLA. *(One third life size.)*

ROCK PINKS AND CERASTIUM IN THE SHADY WALL.

Cardamine trifoliata. They suit admirably as companions to some of the smaller Ferns. The Double Cuckoo-flower (*Cardamine pratensis*) is an excellent wall-plant.

The accommodating *Cruciferæ*, Arabis, Alyssum, and Aubrietia will flower just as freely in the cool as in the warm wall, also the Wallflowers, whether the garden kinds or the species.

An autumn sowing of *Ionopsidium acaule* will give next season a good crop of this charming little plant. *Linaria alpina* can also be sown, and *Erinus alpinus*, which seems willing to grow in any position. Garden Primroses and Anemones are thankful for a place at the cool wall-foot.

PLANTS FOR THE ROCK-WALL IN SHADE

Ferns, native and foreign.
Saxifrages.
Ramondia pyrenaica.
Alpine Auriculas.
Primula involucrata, Allionii, glutinosa, marginata, nivalis, viscosa.
Androsace lanuginosa, carnea, chamæjasme, Laggeri.
Anemone appenina, sylvestris, Hepatica.
Antirrhinum majus (Snapdragon).
Sempervivum, in variety.
Smilacina bifolia.
Acæna microphylla, pulchella.

Lysimachia nummularia (Moneywort).
Corydalis ochroleuca.
Waldsteinia fragarioides.
Campanula carpatica, turbinata, pyramidalis, persicifolia, latifolia, pusilla, cæspitosa.
Symphyandra pendula, Hoffmanni.
Arenaria balearica, montana.
Hutchinsia alpina.
Cardamine trifoliata.
Cardamine pratensis fl. pl.
Ionopsidium acaule (seed).
Linaria alpina (seed).

CHAPTER V

NATIVE PLANTS IN THE ROCK-WALL

WHEN a wall-garden has been established for some years one may expect all kinds of delightful surprises, for wind-blown seeds will settle in the joints and there will spring up thriving tufts of many a garden plant, perhaps of the most unlikely kind. Foxgloves, plants that in one's mind are associated with cool, woody hollows, may suddenly appear in a sunny wall, so may also the great garden Mulleins. When this happens, and the roots travel back and find the coolness of the stone, the plants show astonishing vigour. I had some Mulleins (*Verbascum phlomoides*) that appeared self-sown in a south-west wall; they towered up to a height of over nine feet, and were finer than any others in the garden; while everything that is planted or that sows itself in the wall seems to acquire quite exceptional vigour.

It sometimes happens also that some common native plant comes up in the wall so strongly and flowers so charmingly that one lets it be and is thankful. The illustration (p. 88) shows a case where the wild Stitch-wort (*Stellaria Holostea*) appeared in the wall and was welcomed as a beautiful and desirable plant. Close to this tuft, which has now for five years been one of the

STITCHWORT IN A ROCK-WALL. WELSH POPPY AND HART'S-TONGUE FERN AT FOOT.

best things in the place at its own flowering-time, is a colony, also spontaneous, of the Shining Cranesbill (*Geranium lucidum*), whose glistening, roundish, five-lobed leaves turn almost scarlet towards the end of summer. These are both common hedge-weeds, but so dainty is their structure and kind of beauty that we often pass them by among the coarser herbage of the country lanes and hedges, and only find that they are worthy garden plants when we have them more quietly to ourselves in the rock-wall. There are other wild plants that are also worthy of wall space. The Wall Pennywort (*Cotyledon Umbilicus*), so common in the south-west of England, is a precious plant, and is especially happy in combination with hardy Ferns. *Linaria Cymbalaria* is a gem in a rough wall, and, though a doubtful native, is so generally found as a wild wall-plant that it takes its place in books of British botany. The yellow Toadflax (*Linaria vulgaris*) is also a grand wall-plant, and so is the yellow Corydalis (*C. lutea*), though the paler flowered and more daintily leaved *C. ochroleuca*, is a better plant ; just a good shade more delicate and more beautiful throughout, and in flower all the summer. In considering the best of the native plants for wall-gardening, the Welsh Poppy (*Meconopsis cambrica*) must not be forgotten ; its place is at the foot of a wall, and in its lower courses among Ferns. Nearly all the British Ferns can be grown in walls, many of them acquiring great luxuriance. As nearly all are plants that love shade and coolness and some degree of moisture, they should be in walls

that face east or north; the larger kinds in the
lower joints and quite at the foot, and many of
the smaller ones in the upper joints. The Common
Polypody runs freely along the joints, and the
shelter preserves the fronds from winter injury; so
that often, when severe weather kills the wild ones
in the lanes and hedges, those that have the protection of the wall will carry their fronds, as will
also the Harts-tongue, green and perfect throughout the winter.

It would be well worth having a bit of cool wall
for British plants and Ferns alone; its beauty would
scarcely be less than that of a wall planted with
exotics.

There are two small English Ferns that do not
object to a dry and sunny place, namely, *Asplenium
Ruta-muraria* and *Asplenium Trichomanes.* They
seem to be fond of the lime in the joints of old
mortar-jointed walls, and able to endure almost any
amount of sunshine. Of the other English plants
that like warm wall-treatment three come at once
to mind; all of them plants so good that for
hundreds of years they have been cultivated in
gardens. These are Thrift, Wallflower, and Red
Valerian. In a sunny wall all these will be at
home. Wallflowers never look so well as in a wall,
where air and light is all around them and where
they grow sturdy and stocky, and full of vigour.
Compare a close-growing, bushy Wallflower in a
wall, with its short-jointed, almost woody stem,
stout and unmoved in a gale of wind, with one

planted out in a bed. The garden-nurtured plant will be a foot and a half or two feet high, and its large heavy head will be beaten about and twisted by the wind till it has worked a funnel-shaped hole in the ground, and is perhaps laid flat. Thrift, that lovely little plant of rocky seashore and wind-blown mountain top, is indispensable in all rock and wall gardening, neat and well clothed all through the year, and in summer thickly set with its flower-heads of low-toned pink. It loves in nature to grow along rocky cracks, sending its long neck and root far down among the stones. There is a garden form with bright green leaves and darker coloured flowers, but, though it is un-doubtedly a more showy plant it is scarcely an improvement on the type ; much of the charm is lost.

The Red Valerian (*Centranthus ruber*) is a chalk-loving plant; it will grow in ordinary soil, but is thankful for lime in some form. In this, the garden form of deeper colour is a better plant than the type ; the colour in this case being deepened to a good crimson. Another British plant of the chalk that will also be handsome in the rock-wall is the fine blue-flowered Gromwell (*Lithospermum purpuro-cœruleum*) ; it throws out long runners like a Periwinkle that root at the tips. They seem to feel about over the surface of the wall till they come to a joint where they can root.

Two of the British wild Pinks, namely, *Dianthus cœsius* and *D. deltoides*, are among the best of plants for a sunny wall ; and another, not exactly showy but neat and shrub-like and of considerable interest, well worthy of a warm place, is the Wood Sage (*Teucrium Scorodonia*).

Another charming wild plant for sunny joints and places on a level with the eye, or for such wall-tops as would be only as high as eye level, is the Sheep's Scabious (*Jasione montana*) ; neat and pretty, and worthy of cultivation on wall or dry rock-garden, where the little plants, each with its large flower-head, can be grouped rather more closely than in the heathy wastes where they are generally in a thin sprinkle among short grass. Another plant for wall-top, growing willingly in any soil though preferring lime, is the yellow Rock Rose (*Helianthemum vulgare*), common on sunny banks in chalk districts, and one of the few species (the others rare or local) that are the representatives of the large Cistus tribe of Southern Europe. One more chalk-loving plant should also be in the sunny wall, *Reseda lutea*, the Wild Mignonette ; tall, graceful, and sweet scented. It is best sown in the wall if seed can be obtained.

There are still some native plants for the warm wall of the succulent class. The Houseleek, so frequent on the roof of the cottage outhouse ; the tall and stout *Sedum Telephium*, the Live-Long of old English naming (for a spray of it in a room without water will live a month almost unchanged) ; and the smaller Stonecrops, *S. anglicum, S. album,* and *S. acre.*

There are still to be named for a wild wall in a cool shady place some of our small wood plants ; indeed,

RED VALERIAN IN A DRY-WALL.

they seem never happier than when they become
established in the wall joints and chinks. Such a one
is the Wood Sorrel, one of the daintiest of spring
flowers, whether in wall, garden or wild. Primroses
also take kindly to the lower joints on the shady side,
and the cool wall-foot is the place of all others for one
of the native Irises, *I. fœtidissima*, whose dark green
sword - like leaves are good to see throughout the
winter, while in October the seed-pods are opening
and showing the handsome orange-scarlet fruit.

Then the Purple Columbine is a grand cool wall-
plant ; the delicate yellow-flowered Wood Pimpernel
(*Lysimachia nemorum*) will trail happily in some lower
joints ; the larger Moneywort is one of the best of
wall draperies ; and even two moisture-loving small
things, the Moschatel (*Adoxa*) and the Golden Saxifrage (*Chrysosplenium*) will be satisfied with the coolness of the lowest joints and the comfort of the mossy
wall-foot.

CHAPTER VI

TERRACE AND GARDEN WALLS

A GRAND old wall is a precious thing in a garden, and many are the ways of treating it. If it is an ancient wall of great thickness, built at a time when neither was work shirked nor material stinted, even if many of the joints are empty, the old stone or brick stands firmly bonded, and, already two or three hundred years of age, seems likely to endure well into the future centuries. In such a wall wild plants will already have made themselves at home, and we may only have to put a little earth and a small plant into some cavity, or earth and seed into a narrow open joint, to be sure of a good reward. Often grasses and weeds, rooting in the hollow places, can be raked out and their spaces refilled with better things. When wild things grow in walls they always dispose themselves in good groups ; such groups as without their guidance it would have been difficult to devise intentionally.

So if one had to replant the old moat wall how pleasant a task it would be to rake out the grasses and wild Lettuce and other undesirables, saving the pretty little pale lemon Hawkweed and the Ivy-leaved Toad-flax and the growth of flags by the culvert, and re-placing the weeds with just a few of the plants that

AN OLD MOAT WALL.

might occur in such a place ; among others Wallflower
and Red Valerian and the native Stonecrops. · In such
a wall, which is outside the garden, and seems rather
to belong to the park, it would be suitable to use
these good native plants rather than exotics, such as
would find a more fitting home within garden ground.
A half-double rambling Rose planted inside, and a
wild Clematis, both ramping and bounding over, and
hanging half-way down to the water, would also make
a pleasant break in the long line of the balustrade.

The illustration of a garden terraced in four levels
shows it when recently planted (p. 99). Next the house
the retaining wall is balustraded ; in the lower ones
the path either runs at the foot of the wall or with
only a narrow border on that side, the better to enjoy
the flowers that are planted in the wall joints. Here
are Lavender, Santolina, Catmint, and other plants of
grey foliage, including the tall Mullein, *Verbascum phlomoides.* In a year or two the groups, which show
some scattered units, will have grown together. Here
is the cool backing of the mass of earth, as well as
the root-cooling influence of the stones themselves,
with the exposure to fullest sunshine, that form the
most favourable conditions for such plants. The foreground planting of one of the Megaseas shows the
value of this fine foliage plant next to stone paving.

The repeated terrace always offers special opportunities for good gardening, for whereas the single line of
abrupt change of level, unless treated with some bold-
ness, may in certain aspects have a thin and meagre
appearance ; where it is doubled, there is an oppor-

tunity of treating the two terraces in a much larger way horticulturally, while equally preserving their architectural value.

This richness of effect is plainly seen in the fine example illustrated, though it is open to question whether it would not have been better still had the upper wall been carried solid to the height of the coping of the balustrade, or even higher, and the upper ground levelled up to it(p. 100).

But there are fine things in this piece of gardening. It shows plainly the salutary effect of rambling growths partly veiling the balustrade, and even of tall things of the Cypress class doing the same work, though this came possibly as a happy accident ; such another accident as those that are of so high a value in the tree and shrub overgrowths of the old gardens of Italy.   The defect of arrangement in this picture is a certain monotonous repetition of Gyneriums alternating with Yuccas in the lower border.   Here would have been a grand place for grouping the Yuccas as described in the chapter on the Rock-wall in Sun.

One can hardly imagine a more perfect site for a garden than a place where such an arrangement as this would be reversed on the further side of the lawn, so that there would be a range of double terrace on the shady side as well as on the sunny.   Where new gardens are being made, such a disposition of the ground is well worth considering, for in many sites where ground comes awkwardly with regard to a house—sometimes sloping away diagonally—such a garden could be laid out.

RETAINING WALLS RECENTLY PLANTED.

A DOUBLE TERRACE.

Many a good old garden, not of the earlier times but dating from the latter half of the eighteenth century, has a large space of pleasure ground within walls. When these were planted, wire-netting, that temptingly cheap and useful abomination, had not been invented, iron was a costly commodity, and if the pleasant home grounds were to be given a more permanent fence against deer and cattle than a wooden one, it must needs be a wall. On p. 103 is a wall, broken only by the tall piers of masonry and well-wrought iron gates that lead from the seclusion of the shady garden to the outer world. Where there are fairly long stretches of such walls the artist gardener has good scope for arranging large effects; for doing something thoroughly well and just sufficiently, and then passing on to some other desirable possibility; for making pictures for all the seasons in just such well-considered progression, and just such degree of change or variety as will be most pleasant and delightful to see.

Good walls often have their opportunities wasted. There is generally the usual planting of one each of one thing after another, a wearisome monotony of variety—a sort of exhibition of samples. Where there is little wall-space this may be a kind of necessity, but in these old gardens where the bounding walls run on for many hundred yards, there is no need for any such planting.

Thus one may plant in imagination a long stretch of such wall, beginning at one of the gateways. If the piers are well designed, the first consideration

will be not to let them be smothered by the climbing
plants. One of the many beautiful Ivies, not the
common Irish nor any other of the larger leaved
ones, but such a lovely thing as the dainty Caenwood
variety, is just the thing for the piers, and even this
must be watched and perhaps thinned and suitably
restrained every year or two. Next to it and partly
growing among it, and climbing up one pier, a
Clematis Flammula will do well; its delicate clouds
of bloom lovely in September. Then would come
some darker bushes, *Choisya*, Bay, or Laurustinus,
and next beyond them something totally different;
some pale pink Tree Pæonies grouped with Lavender, and on the wall with this group, which would
be a longish one, the beautiful May-flowering *Clematis montana*, not stiffly trained, but only fastened to
the wall here and there, when its blooming masses
will cling together and hang in grand garlands wide-
swung from point to point; some hanging low so
that they are in close association with the Pæonies,
when one of the year's best flower-pictures will be
to be seen.

Then we will have some garden Roses. The white
Rose (*R. alba*), single and double, and Maiden's
Blush—they are not climbing Roses, but such as
will rise to this wall's height; at their foot will be
more Lavender, and among it bushes of Cabbage
Rose and of Damask and the striped Cottage Maid,
perhaps more commonly known as York and Lan-
caster, a name which, however, belongs of right to
a different Rose of rather the same class. Then we

OLD GARDEN WALL ENCLOSING A SHRUB GARDEN OR WILDERNESS.

would have a good stretch of white Jasmine, sweetest of late summer flowers.

Following this there should be a good length of Guelder Rose, delightful as wall clothing in addition to its usual business as a flowering bush in the open, and at its foot and flowering at the same season will be great clumps of the old crimson Peony. As for Roses, their uses are endless, but for such a wall as this the best will be the free-growing Ayrshires. If any hybrid perpetuals are to have a place they had better be some of the older ones, not now admitted at shows, but such as are often found in old gardens growing on their own roots, and sometimes of great age. They are of the highest value in the garden as the picture (p.107) shows. Such a Rose, though not the one shown, whose name is lost, is Anna Alexeieff; this would be trained free at full length upon the wall—it is not a climber but a free grower—and a group of the same at the foot would be pruned into loose bush form and grouped with the ever-charming Madame Plantier. This combination of pink and white good garden Roses is delightful. One or two Rosemary bushes would be among these, and then a thicker group of Rosemary, some of it trained to the wall. And so on for a good way, with Rosemary and any of the garden Roses that we may love best, and on the wall old favourites like Blairii No. 2, Climbing Captain Christy, and Climbing Aimée Vibert.

Two hundred yards of wall would soon be covered with even this limited choice of kinds, and then it

---

" . . . That simple human need for the solace of a quiet garden, plentifully watered and well furnished with beautiful flowers and foliage and noble tree-form."

OLD OUTER GARDEN WALL.

ONE OF THE OLDER HYBRID PERPETUAL ROSES; NAME LOST.

would be time to change the character of the planting, though perhaps still within the Rose family, so
that next we might have that pretty thornless Tree
Bramble *Rubus deliciosus*, and below it some of the
other unarmed Brambles, the rosy *R. odoratus* and
the white *R. nutkanus*. Then there might come a
stretch of wall for winter bloom ; the yellow Winter
Jasmine (*J. nudiflorum*) and Winter Sweet (*Chimonanthus fragrans*) and *Garrya elliptica ;* the evergreen
branches of the *Garrya* partly protecting the naked
bloom of the *Chimonanthus*.

These are only a few of the combinations that
might be made ; while long lengths of wall may
well be given to Vines, with Lilies and Irises at their
foot, and with here and there a thin climber such
as one of the large-flowered Clematises, or *Rhodochiton volubile*, to run among their branches. For
gate-piers of wrought stone that are in still more
dressed ground nothing is more suitable than that
splendid climber, the best form of *Bignonia radicans*,
but it is too tender for the cold midlands.

When a garden prospect embraces the view of an
ancient building it seems to reduce the range of choice
to within much narrower limits. In the garden shown
in the picture this has evidently been felt, in that here
is a good planting of the June-flowering Pæonies and
nothing much else. Had it suited the other needs of
the garden as well, it might have been even better to
have planted large masses of sober greenery, as of Yew
and Box, with no other flowers than some bold clumps
of white Lilies and a few bushes of white Roses, and

RUBUS DELICIOSUS.

A PEONY BORDER IN RELATION TO OLD BUILDINGS

perhaps some Rosemary and China Rose or some other old garden Rose of tender pink colouring. But the bold forms of the flower and the important leafage of the Peonies are good here also; the only thing that is unworthy of the scheme being the small row of Pansies next the grass. It would have been better to let the Peonies bush over the edge of the grass; the row of small flowers is a petty intrusive incident in a scene where nothing should sound any note that jars upon the harmony of noble ancient building and simple dignity of garden practice.

The gardener may represent that, when masses of foliage of large herbaceous plant or shrub hang over the grass, it is difficult to mow to the edge — and to a certain degree he is right. It is undoubtedly easier to run the machine along a clearly defined and unobstructed edge. But if the gardener is the good fellow that he generally is he will at once understand that this is just one of the points that makes the difference between the best and most careful and thoughtful gardening, and gardening that is ease-loving and commonplace. In the case of such edges, instead of a man and a boy with a mowing-machine the man has a scythe and the boy has a bean-pole. Boy and man face each other a few paces apart, the boy moves backward, lifting the foliage with his pole, while the man advances mowing under the held-up leaves. There is nothing in it that the plainest labourer cannot understand, while the added refinement that is secured is a distinct gain to the garden. It is only where the labour allowed is already insufficient that the gardener's plea should be allowed.

Nothing is more frequently to be seen, even in quite good and well-manned gardens, than this tyranny of the turf-edge. An attempt should always be made to combine beauty and utility by having the turf-edge neither too straight nor too overgrown by the foliage of the inmates of the border. In the accompanying illustration can be seen a happy mean.

The illustration of another flower border in the same good garden as the one with the Peonies, where all things seem to be so well done that there is little that can be criticised, shows the better way of letting the plants lap over the broad grass verge. Here is a wall about twelve feet high, with a noble flower border at its foot. Already it has an old growth of Ivy, while the young Magnolia towards the front, when it has had a few more years of growth, will repeat the mass of deep green foliage. Then its own great leaves will just suggest that larger scale of permanent foliage that will better suit the height of the wall. Wisely has the border been planted with just the very best things ; with Delphinium and white Lily in generous masses, and bold groups of Flag-leaved Irises and bountiful clumps of Pinks. When the Roses on the wall have come to their strength and the Pillar Roses have covered their poles, this flower border will be a fine example of good hardy gardening.

A BORDER WHOSE BRIEF EDGE IS NEITHER TOO STRAIGHT NOR TOO OVERGROWN.

A WELL-PLANTED WALL AND HARDY FLOWER-BORDER NOT YET MATURED:

CHAPTER VII

TERRACE AND GARDEN WALLS (*continued*)

To any one who has both practised and studied gardening for a number of years, and has at last acquired a
glimmering of illumination as to what is best to be
done in the many circumstances presented by various
sites, it is immensely instructive to see gardens or even
to see pictures of them. Perhaps the pictures are
even the best, if there are enough of one place to give
an idea of all its portions, or if there are several illustrations of some important feature. In the black and
white presentment of a scene, that can be held in the
hand and examined quietly and at leisure, without the
distractions of brilliant sunshine or colour, or wind or
rain, or the company of one's fellow-creatures (however charming and sympathetic they may be), the
merits of the scene can be very fairly judged. It may
therefore be useful to make a few remarks on a definite piece of gardening; an important wall-garden in a
fine place in Somerset. The four*pictures give an
accurate idea of the steeply terraced garden. The first
shows both terraces, with a glimpse of the walk on the
third or lowest level, and the still steeply sloping grass
below. The next two pictures show the middle level,
looking both ways from nearly midway in its length.

* Note to 1982 edition. It would appear that, during the preparation of one
of the many editions of this book, two of the 'four pictures' were removed.
Of the remaining two shown here, one seems to be that referred to below:
"The first shows both terraces. . .and the still steeply sloping grass below"
(see p. 117), while the other, shown on p. 118, is the subject of comments
on p. 119.

The upper terrace shows not unskilful manage-
ment of a rather abrupt transition from the wooded
slope to pure formality by a nearly symmetrical line
of evergreens. Next comes a grand retaining wall,
buttressed at short intervals and planted with good
wall-shrubs. The wall rises enough to form a parapet
to the upper terrace. The point where each buttress
rises and gives occasion to widen the coping above,
is accentuated by an American Aloe in a pot. The
pots are of plain flower-pot shape and look a little
too plain for this use, although the character of the
walling does not demand vases highly enriched.

The weakest point in the middle terrace is the
poverty of scheme in the succession of small square
beds that break forward in each bay between the
piers, and that seem to be planted without any general
design or distinct intention, but with stiff little edgings showing an outer margin of bare earth. This
would be much improved by putting all the beds
together as to the space nearest the wall ; and, next
the grass, by leaving the length of the front edge
of two beds and the interval between them, and in
the space represented by the front of the third, swing-
ing the front line back in an arc (not a whole semi-
circle but something shallower), in the centre of
which the pot plants would stand ; then continuing
the treatment with the next pair of beds, followed
by the segmental swing-back, and so on throughout.
Moreover, the front line of the beds comes too far
forward into the grass by about one-fourth of its
projection, taken from the line of the front of the

A TERRACED GARDEN ON A STEEP SOUTHERN SLOPE. (*No.* I.)

LOWER TERRACE. (*No. 2.*)

buttresses. The proportion would be much better with a greater width of grass and a lesser width of flowers.

The little fountain basin would then make a reversed figure in one of the arcs, and the planting on each side of it would be symmetrical and rather important. Such a rearrangement of the beds would much improve this terrace ; and would give the wall added dignity and offer more scope for the growing of handsome groups of plants.

The Yew hedge which forms the parapet of this terrace and stands just at the top of the lowest wall is a capital example of its kind, though the garden would have given a better impression of cohesion if the wall had been treated in the same way as the one above. But the planting at its base seems in these more horticulturally enlightened days to be quite indefensible. The foot of one of the noblest ranges of terrace walls in England is too good to be given over to the most commonplace forms of bedding, whereas it presents the best and most becoming site for some of the most important plants ; for *Magnolia* and *Bignonia*, *Yucca*, *Carpenteria*, *Choisya*, and *Romneya*. Here it would be better to have a much narrower border against the wall, about half the width of the present one, and to take some advantage of the open joints in the upper courses for the planting of some of the lovely things named in the chapter on the Sunny Rock-wall.

Perhaps I should offer some apology to the owners of this fine garden for my presumption in making it an object-lesson ; but the many evidences of good gardening it displays seem an encouragement to the making of friendly criticism. It is already so good that it is tempting to contemplate how such a combination of pleasant conditions could be made even better or be differently treated.

Where there is beautiful architectural proportion and enriched detail, as in the example of the portion of a fine old Tudor house shown in the illustration, it is obvious that it would be most unwise to let it be over-run with coarse or common creepers. In this case there is evidence of watchful restraint; the climbing plants are just enough to clothe sufficiently, while none of the beauty of the building is unduly hidden.

The whole question of the relation of vegetation to architecture is a very large one, and to know what to place where, and when to stop, and when to abstain altogether, requires much knowledge on both sides. The horticulturist generally errs in putting his plants and shrubs and climbers everywhere, and in not even discriminating between the relative fitness of any two plants whose respective right use may be quite different and perhaps even antagonistic. The architect, on the other hand, is often wanting in sympathy with beautiful vegetation. The truth appears to be that for the best building and planting, where both these crafts must meet and overlap and work together, the architect and the gardener must have *some* knowledge of each other's business, and each must regard with

*RESTRAINED USE OF CREEPERS ON AN OLD HOUSE THAT HAS
BEAUTIFUL ARCHITECTURAL DETAILS.*

CAMPANULA PYRAMIDALIS, ETC., IN THE JOINTS OF STONE STEPS.

feelings of kindly reverence the unknown domains of the other's higher knowledge. By the gardener is not meant the resident servant, but the person, whoever it may be, who works with or directly after the architect in planning the planting.

The terraces just described have so little of special architectural design that they may be considered as belonging entirely to the garden, so that there is no reason why they may not be treated with absolute freedom.

One of the careful gardener's duties is to watch, not the growth only, but the overgrowth of plants, trees, and shrubs. In many a garden some overgrowth of shrub or tree may be of the highest pictorial value. Sometimes wild plants will come in stonework and come just right, or seeds of garden plants will find lodgment in a crack or joint of masonry, and provide some new or attractive feature that had never been thought of. Often Ferns and small wild things will grow in the joints of walls and steps on any cool exposure. It is well worth while to notice the willingness of plants to grow in such places, and to encourage or restrain as may be needful. In the wide stone steps of the Gloucestershire house with the pedimented doorway are some seedling plants of several ages of the handsome white Chimney Campanula (*C. pyramidalis*); it also grows spontaneously in the wall of a shallow area to the basement of the same building. In these steps the growth of this and other plants has been encouraged. They are perhaps rather more scattered all over the

steps than is desirable. The sentiment conveyed by a shallow flight is one of welcome and easy access, and it is best that no plants should be allowed to invade the middle space, or at any rate none so large that they rise to the height of a single step. But the presence of such plants gives a keen delight to the flower lover, even though his sympathies with architecture may tell him that for plants to be in such a place is technically wrong. This picture calls to mind the story of how the common Harebell (*Campanula rotundifolia*) is said to have come by the specific name that seems so little descriptive of the very narrow leaves of the flower-stalks, though the less noticeable root leaves are roundish. It is said that Linnæus observed it as a little round-leaved plant, growing in the joints of the steps of the University of Upsala, and named it from its rounded foliage of winter and spring.

The Ivy-leaved Toadflax is a charming plant in the joints of steps, and so are some of the smaller Campanulas, such as *cæspitosa* and *pusilla*, and even some rather larger kinds, as *turbinata* and *carpatica*.

In the other example of weed and grass-grown steps, the overgrowth needs restraining and regulating. The lowest of the six steps badly wants the shears, and the invasion of the small-leaved Ivy, which would be desirable if not quite so thick, is also complicated and made to look untidy by many tufts of grass that would be much better away(p. 126).

The Scotch walled garden, with its fine row of

"*Where there is a stream passing through. . . a garden, there will be a happy prospect of delightful ways of arranging and enjoying the beautiful plants that love wet places. Even where there are no natural advantages. . . given a little sinking of the level and the least trickle of water, with a simple and clever arrangement of bold groups of suitable plants, a pretty stream-picture may be made.*"

GARDEN STEPS, TOO MUCH OVERGROWN.

IVY-LEAFED TOAD FLAX, IN THE JOINTS OF BRICK GARDEN STEPS.

GROUPING OF TREE AND GARDEN WALL IN A SCOTCH GARDEN.

Pansies, shows the value of good groups of trees in connection with walls.

There is many a dismal wall, or court with paving right up to the wall, where the clever placing of some suitable plant in a chink of broken-cornered flag-stone, or empty joint close to the wall-foot, may redeem the dulness and want of interest of such a region of unbroken masonry. The plants most suitable for such a place are Male Fern and Harts-tongue, Welsh Poppy, and *Iris fœtidissima ;* all but the Poppy having also the advantage of winter beauty. Just lately in my own home I have had an example of the willingness of a pretty plant to grow in the little space offered by the meeting of two paving-stones, one of which had lost an angle. Here a seed of *Mimulus cupreus* grew self-sown, and the neat little plant, with its rich, deep orange bloom flowering all the summer, is a joy to see. This would also be a plant for the stone-paved sunless court with others of its family, including the common Musk.

The picture(p.130)of a stone bridge in the north of England shows how much a good and simple structure gains by the invasion of Ivy and wild things of even more bushy growth. Here is a beneficent piece of human work in a naturally beautiful landscape of wood and water. Stream and forest accept the man-wrought bridge and offer it welcome and brother-hood by adorning it with the friendly growths, whose masses are so admirably disposed, that the scene

BRIDGE WITH WILD OVERGROWTH, SHOWING A GOOD COMBINATION OF MASONRY AND VEGETATION.

A TERRACE WALL CLOTHED WITH CASCADES OF LAVENDER.

becomes a picture that is very much the better for the presence of the bridge, while the bridge itself is much the more beautiful for the neighbourly invasion.

The same influence of vegetation in softening the aspect of rugged architecture may be seen wherever there are old buildings; its presence investing the ancient structure with a whole new range of qualities that excite the keenest interest in cultivated minds. For who can see the splendid work of human design and skill as shown in this grand rough-hewn masonry, absolutely adapted to its own work, and yet, from its complete sympathy with surrounding nature, seeming to grow spontaneously out of the rocky gorge; who can see this, made all the more perfect by the lovely work of God in the dainty Fern fronds of the Maidenhair, without a thrill of humble admiration and thankfulness?

CHAPTER VIII

SOME PROBLEMS IN WALL-GARDENING

THE illustration shows one of the many pleasant ways in which a little careful study of ground problems and ingenious adaptation of material can be worked out and made into a simple thing of beauty and delight (p. 135).

A half-sunk garden passage leads on a gentle uphill slope from house to stables. The walls are of blocks of stone with wide joints, all laid a little sloping back, so that the whole face of the two walls lies back. The wall was planted, both as it was built, and also afterwards, with quantities of spring-flowering plants; Arabis, Aubrietia, Violets, Pinks, Cerastium, and others of early bloom. The crowning pergola, on which grow Vines only (late-leafing in England), does not over-shade the early flowers when they are in bloom, while later it rather gives them comfort by sheltering them from the summer sun-heat. The path is paved with flags so that it neither wants weeding nor repair from being washed out, while the very easiest sweeping keeps it clean.

Many are the unsightly and featureless places that by some such treatment might be made beautiful, and more quickly than in any other way of gardening;

133

for the wall-plants having their roots always cool seem
to grow away quickly at once, and yet to be longer-
lived than their own brother plants in the more level
garden.

Indeed, wall-gardening is not only extremely interesting and soon rewarding, but it seems to quicken
the inventive faculty ; for if one has once tasted its
pleasures and mastered some of the simpler ways of
adapting it for use, others are sure to present themselves, and a whole new region of discursive delights
offers itself for the mental exploration of the horticulturally inventive. One after another, pleasant
schemes come to mind, soon to be fashioned, with
careful design and such manual skill as may have
been acquired, into such simple things of beauty
and delight as this first flower-walled and then Vine-
shaded pleasant pathway.

Besides the wall-gardening that may be designed
and reared, there is also that which is waiting to be
done in walls that are already in being. Sometimes
there is an old wall from whose joints the surface
mortar has crumbled and fallen. Such a wall as is
shown in the illustration is indeed a treasure, for its
rugged surface can soon be jewelled with the choicest
of mural vegetation (p. 136).

But so good a chance is not for every garden, for
often the wall that one would wish to make the home
of many a lovely plant is of the plainest brick or stone,
and the mortar joints are fairly sound. Still the ardent
wall-gardener is not to be daunted, for, armed with a
hammer and a bricklayer's cold chisel, he knocks out

AN OUTDOOR FLAGGED PASSAGE WITH PLANTS IN DRY-WALL AND PERGOLA OVER.

AN OLD WALL WITH OPEN JOINTS, WELL ADAPTED TO WALL GARDENING.

joints and corners of bricks (when a builder is not looking on) exactly where he wishes to have his ranges of plants.

A well-built wall, seasoned and solidified by some years' standing, will bear a good deal of such knocking about. In chiselling out the holes the only thing that had better be avoided is making much of a cavity just under an upright joint; nor is it ever needful, for even if one wishes to have a longish range of any one plant, shown in the diagram (p. 139) in the case of growth horizontally hatched, the plants will close up, though planted in the first place a little way apart, while there is nothing against widening any upright joint or making it gape funnelwise either upward or down.

The diagram gives a general indication of the way in which it is advised that plants should be disposed. It shows four kinds in a section of wall of from six to seven feet long. Three of the kinds are hatched across in different ways to distinguish them. Even this sort of arrangement would be monotonous unless it were varied by some wall spaces left almost blank, and then perhaps with one such range alone. The four kinds are almost too many at a time, and were only crowded in to illustrate the same kind of arrangement with slight variations. The way of growth must, of course, be taken into account, for it would be a grievous oversight to plant a range of Rock Pinks or Arabis or Alyssum, that in a year or two will hang down two feet, and to plant in the next course below them some other smaller things that would soon be smothered. So the upright growth of Wallflower, Snapdragon, and

Valerian must be considered and allowed for as well as the down-drooping of those that make hanging sheets. So also the neat stay-at-home habit of Thrift will be taken into account, and the way of running along a joint of Polypody and *Campanula cæspitosa*.

From March to May, or just after they ripen in the autumn, seeds are put in mixed with a little loamy earth, and if the cleft or opening is an upright one, unwilling to retain the mixture, a little stone is wedged in at the bottom or even cemented in. For a plant of rather large growth, like Valerian (*Centranthus*), a whole coping brick can be knocked off the top, and probably quite a nice rooting-place be made with the downward digging chisel, to be filled up with suitable soil.

By some such means, and always thinking and trying and combining ideas, the plainest wall can in a couple of years be so pleasantly transformed that it is turned into a thing of flowery beauty. There is no wall with exposure so hot or so cold that has not a plant waiting for just the conditions that it has to offer, and there will be no well-directed attempt to convert mural ugliness into beauty whose result will not be an encouragement to go on and do still better.

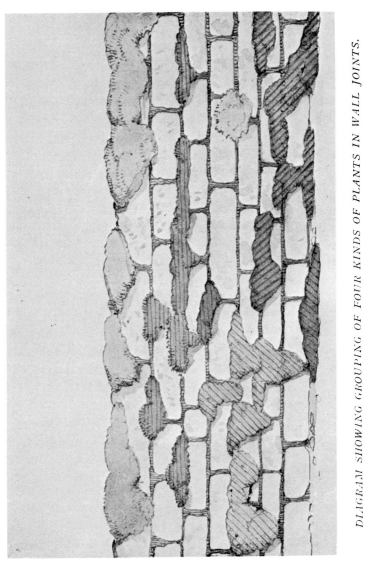

DIAGRAM SHOWING GROUPING OF FOUR KINDS OF PLANTS IN WALL JOINTS.

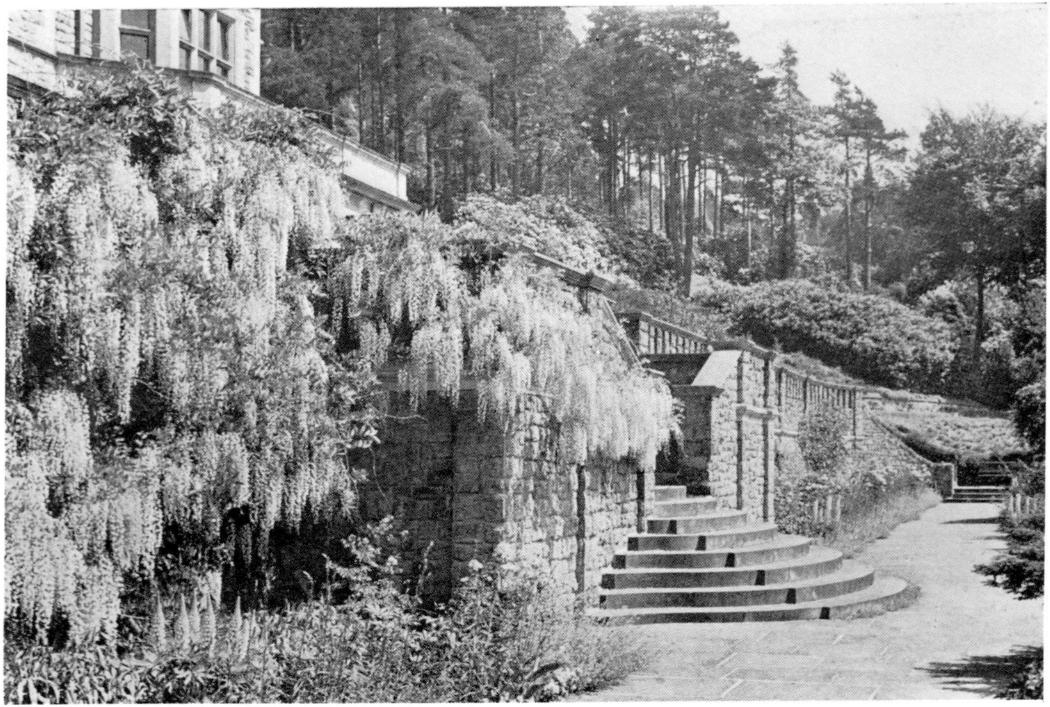

WISTARIA ON A TERRACE WALL.

CHAPTER IX

WHEN TO LET WELL ALONE

In garden arrangement, as in all other kinds of decorative work, one has not only to acquire a knowledge of what to do, but also to gain some wisdom in perceiving what it is well to let alone. The want of such knowledge or discrimination, or whatever it may be called, is never more frequently or more conspicuously shown than in the treatment of grassy spaces in pleasure grounds, that are planted at the discretion of some one who has not the gift of knowing what kind of placing, of what trees or shrubs, is the most advisable.

Such a one naturally says, " Here is a space of turf otherwise unoccupied, let us put there a specimen tree." It may be a place in which the careful and highly cultured garden critic may say, " Here is a space of turf, let us be thankful for it, and above all things guard it from any intrusion." I call to mind two good places where there is a dignified house, and groups of grand trees, and stretches of what should be unbroken level sward. In older days it was so ; the spreading branches of the great Cedars and Beeches came down to the lawn, and on summer evenings the shadow of a noble grove of ancient trees swept clear across the grassy level. The whole picture was perfect in its unity and peace, in its harmony of line and fine masses of form—full of dignity, repose, and abounding satisfaction.

Now the smooth lawn-levels have been broken by a dotting about of specimen Conifers. One *Abies nordmanniana*, one Thuya, one Wellingtonia, one Araucaria, one Taxodium, and so on, and so on. What once was a sanctuary of ordered peace is now a wearisome and irritating exposition of monotonous commonplace. The spiritual and poetical influences of the garden are gone. The great Cedars are still there, but from no moderately distant point can they now be seen because of the impertinent interposition of intruding " specimens."

Like many another thing done in gardens, how much better it would have been not to have done it; to have left the place unspoilt and untormented by these disastrous interlopers. If only it had just been let alone !

The illustration (p. 144) shows a house in South Middle England. The picture is complete. The great building is reflected in the still water, and the natural water margin, without any artificial planting, is wisely let alone. It is all so solemn, so dignified, that any added fussiness of small detail, however beautiful in itself, would be a kind of desecration. There are plenty of other opportunities for gardening about this fine place, already wisely treated, and though it is tempting to plant any edge of pool or

THALICTRUM DIPTEROCARPUM AT THE WATERSIDE.

A FINE HOUSE, WITH UNBROKEN LAWN SPACE AND QUIET WATER-EDGE.

river, happily it has those for its owners who, with wise discrimination, see that it is better undisturbed.

So again in the case of a wild forest pool, such as the one in the picture (p. 146). Here is a glimpse of quiet natural beauty; pure nature untouched. Being in itself beautiful, and speaking direct to our minds of the poetry of the woodland, it would be an ill deed to mar its perfection by any meddlesome gardening. The most one could do in such a place, where deer may come down to drink and the dragon-fly flashes in the broken midsummer light, would be to plant in the upper ground some native wild flower that would be in harmony with the place but that may happen to be absent, such as Wood Sorrel or Wood Anemone; but nothing that would recall the garden. Here is pure forest, and garden should not intrude. Above all, the water-margin should be left as it is. Foreign Irises, so good to plant by many garden pools, would here be absurd and only painfully obtrusive, and as the place is already right it is far best let alone. There are many places that call aloud for judicious planting. This is one where all meddling is forbidden. The beauty and dignity of some ancient monastic ruin is often marred and the whole thing vulgarized by disastrous gardening. Such a place should be let alone; only beds of nettles or any growths of distinctly unpleasant effect should be carefully removed.

A WOOD POOL BEST LET ALONE.

CHAPTER X

THE STREAM-GARDEN AND MARSH POOLS

WHERE there is a stream passing through the outskirts of a garden, there will be a happy prospect
of delightful ways of arranging and enjoying the
beautiful plants that love wet places. Even where
there are no natural advantages of pictorial environment, given a little sinking of the level and the least
trickle of water, with a simple and clever arrangement of bold groups of suitable plants, a pretty
stream-picture may be made, as is seen by the illustration of the water-garden in a good nursery near
London.

But where there is a rather wider and more copious
stream, rippling merrily over its shallow bed, there
are even wider possibilities. The banks of running
water where the lovely Water Forget-me-not grows
are often swampy, and the path that is to be carried
near one of them may probably want some such treatment as is recommended in the early part of the
chapter on Water Margins. When a water-garden is
being prepared by the side of any such stream, the
course of the path may well be varied by running first
close beside the water and then retreating a yard or two

inland ; then it might cross on stepping-stones and again run inland and perhaps pass behind a little knoll and then again come back to the stream. Then the stream might divide, and the path be carried between two rills, and so on in a progression of varied incident that would be infinitely more interesting than if the path kept to one bank nearly always at the same distance from the water after the manner of a towing-path.

I am supposing my stream to run along the bottom of a little valley. Close to it the ground is open, except for a few tufts of low wild bushes. As the ground rises it is wooded, first with sparse copse-wood and groups of Birches and Hollies ; and after this with a rather thick wood of Scotch Fir.

Having pleasantly diversified the path in relation to the stream, we have to think how best it may be planted. Some of the plants suited to the running stream edge will be the same as for the margins of stiller ponds, but some that have a liking for running water will be proper to the stream itself. Such a one is the Water Forget-me-not. If it does not occur in the neighbourhood it is easy to raise quite a large stock from seed ; and strong seedlings or divisions of older plants have only to be planted in the muddy soil at the water edge when they will soon grow into healthy spreading sheets and give plenty of the dainty bloom whose blue is the loveliest of any English plant. Next to the Forget-me-not on the water edge, and also a little more inland, I should plant the double Meadow-

ASTILBES AT THE STREAM EDGE.

Sweet, the double garden form of the wild *Spiræa Ulmaria*, and again beyond it, quite out of sight of the Forget-me-not, others of the herbaceous Spiræas, *S. palmata*, *S. venusta*, and *S. Aruncus*—all moisture-loving plants. Drifts of these might spread away inland, the largest of them, which would be of *Spiræa Aruncus*, being placed the furthest from the stream; they are plants of bold aspect, showing well at a little distance.

I should be careful not to crowd too many different plants into my stream-picture. Where the Forget-me-nots are it would be quite enough to see them and the double Meadow-Sweet, and some good hardy moisture-loving Fern, Osmunda or Lady Fern. The way to enjoy these beautiful things is to see one picture at a time ; not to confuse the mind with a crowded jumble of too many interesting individuals, such as is usually to be seen in a water-garden.

Close by the stream-side and quite out of view of other flowering plants should be a bold planting of *Iris lævigata*, the handsome Japanese kind, perhaps better known as *Iris Kæmpferi*. It is in varied colourings of white, lilac, and several shades and kinds of purple ; but for this stream, where it is desirable to have the simplest effects, the single pure white alone will be best. There are double varieties, but in these the graceful purity of the form is lost and the character of the flower is confused. The best way to grow them in England is in the boggy margin, not in the stream itself; for though seeds will fall and germinate in shallow water, planted roots do better just out of it, but always with their heads in the full sunshine. This is one of the many cases where the natural ways of a plant cannot be followed in our gardens, for in Japan they commonly grow with the roots submerged. Some plants of bright green foliage, such as the handsome branched Bur-reed (*Sparganium ramosum*) will fittingly accompany groups of this noble Water Iris.

The yellow Mimulus (*M. luteus*) is a capital thing for the stream-side; once planted it will take care of itself; indeed it has become naturalised by many streams in England. Another interesting and pretty plant that would do well in its company is the only English representative of the Balsams, *Impatiens Noli-me-tangere;* it is an annual, but will sow itself again.

It should be noted that in such a stream-garden it will usually be the opposite side that is best seen, and this should be borne in mind while composing the pictures and setting out the path.

It is well worth while to consider some pleasant arrangement of colour in the way the varied flower-pictures will present themselves in the course of a walk; thus, after the blue Forget-me-not with the white Spiræas might come the pink and rosy colourings of *Spiræa venusta* and *S. palmata*.

As the stream leads further away we begin to forget

the garden, and incline towards a wish for the beautiful things of our own wilds, so that here would be, for the earliest water flowers of the year, the smaller of the wild kinds of Water Buttercup (*Ranunculus aquatilis*). The larger kind, more frequent near London, *R. grandiflorus*, is figured on p. 257. The smaller one is in better proportion to the size of the little stream. The picture shows how it grows in pretty patches, though the stream is not the one that is being described. Near it, but flowering later, are some strong patches of the native yellow Water Iris (*I. Pseud-acorus*), some of the same being in a swampy patch a yard or two from the bank on the other side of the path, with some of the handsome smooth-leaved rank growth of the Water Dropwort.

A little further the tall yellow Loosestrife (*Lysimachia*) will make some handsome patches; then will come a few yards of rest from bright flowers and a region of Fern-fringed stream bank, where the Lady Fern, one of the most delicately beautiful of waterside plants, should have a good space; some plants almost touching the water and others a little way up the bank.

After this the character of the stream shows a change, for here is a clump of Alders, the advance guard of a greater number that are to be seen beyond. Now it is time to make some important effect with plants of a larger size, that will prepare the eye, as it were, for the larger scale of the water-

IRIS LÆVIGATA OR KAEMPFERI, AS IT GROWS IN JAPAN.

loving trees. Here, therefore, we have a widespread planting of these large things. By the stream on one bank a long-shaped mass of the rosy Loosestrife (*Lythrum*), and detached patches of the same handsome plant, and grouped near and partly with it the Giant Cow-Parsnip (*Heracleum*). The one so long in cultivation is a grand plant in such a place, but still better is the newer *H. mantegazzianum*. On the other bank is the native Butter-bur (*Petasites*) with its immense leaves, a striking contrast in leaf-form to its neighbours.

Now the stream passes into the swampy region of Willow and Alder, and the path follows it only a little way in; but already we have been among great clumps of Marsh Marigold, some close down to the stream edge in the open, and some in wet hollows a yard or two away. But in the dark pools of mud and water under the Alders the clumps grow larger and more luscious, and in April they are a sight to see, showing sheets of rich yellow bloom, that look all the brighter rising alone from the black pools under the trees.

The path that has hitherto accompanied the stream now turns away from it, and on its return journey skirts the streamward side of some boggy pools and oozy places that lie at the foot of the wood's edge. The wood is mostly of Scotch Fir, with a lesser number of Oaks, Hollies, and Birches in the opener parts. It slopes down to the little valley, ending in a ragged line of low scarp never more than four feet high, showing dark peaty earth, and below it whitish or yellowish sand more or less stained by the darker soil above. The drainage from the wooded hill seems to gather in the chain of pool and swamp at the foot. The pools lie perhaps two feet above the level of the stream ; here and there a sort of natural shallow ditch carries the water into it from them. The water seems to drain out of the hill very slowly, for nowhere does it run, and only near the stream, which is about fifty yards away, can one sometimes hear a tiny trickle. It is an ideal place for a wild garden of plants that like boggy ground and cool wood-side places. The wood rises to the south-west, so that the marshy region is mostly in shade. Between this boggy belt and the stream is rough grass and a few low thorn bushes and brambles, in ground which is not exactly marshy, but always cool and damp.

Some of the Firs that come down to the very edge of the wood stand on the low scarp of blackish sandy-looking ground. Here and there it is broken down into a little gently-sloping bank that sucks up the moisture from below and is sunless from the shading of the wood. These little banks, naturally mossy, are just the place for *Linnæa*, and for *Pyrola* and *Trientalis*, three plants of a nature that is neither large nor showy, but that have that charm that cannot be described; that makes the heart leap, and frames the lips into the utterance of an exclamation of joy and thankfulness, and that holds the mind enthralled by the subdued and mysterious poetry of beauty that is a character of these lovely little modest growths of the woodland wilds of our own and other lands.

Here too, rather more in the open, is the Mountain Avens (*Dryas octopetala*), and in that moist hollow, almost swampy and always somewhat in shade, is *Epigæa repens*, the May-flower of New England. Then in the damp grass, more towards the stream, there are here and there tufts of the two Marsh Orchids with flowers of greenish purple, and handsome clear-cut foliage, the Marsh Helleborine and the broad-leaved Helleborine (*Epipactis palustris* and *E. latifolia*).

In a place like this these beautiful things can be seen and enjoyed at ease, and far better than when they are cramped close together in a smaller space. Here again will be the marsh-loving Ferns, and foremost among them great groups of the Royal Fern (Osmunda) at the edge of one of the small marshy pools that are deeply fringed and sometimes filled with the pale-green bog-moss Sphagnum.

These little still pools, some of them only a yard or two across, are not stagnant, for they are constantly fed by the trickle of the springs; and the moisture—scarcely running water—finds its slow way to the stream. Their fringes are a paradise for Ferns. Besides the Royal Fern there are two of the largest and most graceful of British Ferns, *Asplenium Filix-fœmina* and *Nephrodium dilatatum* (Dilated Shield Fern), and

CYPRIPEDIUM SPECTABILE.

down at the moistest pool edge are *Nephrodium Thelypteris* and *Lomaria*, and a little way up on the cool bank, always in shade, the North American *Onoclea sensibilis*. In a moist nook already filled with Sphagnum, in this region of Fern beauty, and with the dusky wood beyond, is a considerable planting of the North American Mocassin-flower (*Cypripedium spectabile*), with its great pouched and winged flowers of rose and white, and its fine plaited leaves of bright fresh green. What a plant! Its beauty almost takes away one's breath. Any one who had never seen it before, suddenly meeting it in such a place, with no distraction of other flower-forms near, would think it was some brilliant stove Orchid escaped into the wild. It loves to throw its long cord-like roots out into black peaty mud, when they will grow strong and interlace into a kind of vegetable rook's-nest. Every year the tufts will become stronger and send up still nobler spikes of leaf and bloom.

Such a sight seems to give the mind a kind of full meal of enjoyment of flower beauty, and it is well that following it there shall be some plant of quite another class. So the next boggy patch has another American plant of a very different form, the curious *Sarracenia purpurea*; a weird, half-hooded trumpet of a thing, of a dull-green colour, closely veined with red purple, and near it, in striking contrast to its mysterious aspect, the frank and pure-looking Grass of Parnassus (*Parnassia palustris*), with its white bloom daintily veined with green and its pretty pearl-like buds. Near

GALAX APHYLLA. (*See page 162.*)

these may also be *Pinguicula grandiflora*, the finest of the native Butterworts, that grows in the bogs of the south-west of Ireland, and looks like handsome Violets rising from the pale-green bog-moss.

One spot of Sphagnum-haunted bog-land should have some of the native marsh plants that are perfect gems of beauty. The little Bog Pimpernel, whose small pink flowers remind one of those of *Linnæa*, the more so that they are generally borne in pairs, though of different habit, in that they stand up instead of drooping. Then there will be the Ivy-leaved Bell-flower, smallest of its kind, its flowers carried on hair-like stalks, and its little leaves of tenderest tissue, Ivy-like with pointed lobes. Then the small Cornish Moneywort (*Sibthorpia europæa*), not hardy in the north, with pretty tender pale-green leaves and flowers scarcely noticeable ; and here may be grown the two little native Bog Orchids, *Malaxis* and *Liparis*. All these are such small things that they might easily be overlooked unless one knew that in such a special place they were to be found for a little searching.

At a place where the bank between wood and marsh is cool and moist, yet not boggy, will be *Gaultheria procumbens*, closely carpeting the ground with its neat sheets of green lighted up by its bright red berry, and above it and stretching in under the Firs its larger relative, *Gaultheria Shallon*. On some cool mossy bank there will be two charming little

XEROPHYLLUM ASPHODELOIDES.

plants, one native, one North American—*Goodyera repens*, with its brightly veined and marbled leaves, creeping close to the ground, where it may have to be looked for among the moss, and *Mitchella repens*, the Partridge Berry. This little plant also creeps among the moss. It has neat entire leaves veined with white, and bright red berries following whitish flowers.

Another plant from North America, a strange, handsome thing that deserves to be better known, will have a place in this region. Out of bloom it would never be noticed among its neighbouring clumps of Royal Fern, for it looks only like a tuft of grass; but when it throws up its tall flower-spikes, *Xerophyllum* is a plant that commands admiration and even some surprise. It flourishes in a peaty place that is cool and damp though not swampy. Another plant of considerable beauty, *Galax aphylla*, likes exactly the same conditions, with a little shade added. This is another of the good things that has come to us from North America, and is a precious plant in several ways of gardening; it is so neat and pretty that it is suitable as a single plant among the choicest things in a restricted collection, while in the wild garden it is equally in place in considerable masses. It thrives where there is peat or sandy leaf-mould that can always be kept a little moist, and though rather slow at first, yet as soon as the tufts begin to grow strongly they increase, spreading outwards, fairly fast. The flowers are gracefully carried on thin, strong, almost wire-like stems, and the leaves, tough and leathery, though not thick, assume a beautiful winter colouring.

Some charming native bog-plants must also not be neglected. The Bog Asphodel (*Narthecium*), with its straight spikes of yellow bloom and neat sheaves of small Iris-like leaves ; the Cotton Grass (*Eriophorum*), and the Sundew (*Drosera rotundifolia*). These all thrive in beds of Sphagnum.

Here also should be the bog-loving Heath (*Erica Tetralix*), the Pink Bell Heather, and its white variety, and our native Sweet Bog Myrtle. Sweeter still and here in place will be the Canadian Candleberry Gale (*Myrica cerifera*), and another of the same most fragrant-leaved family, *Comptonia asplenifolia*, the "Sweet Fern" of the Northern States.

One little marsh pool must be given to *Calla palustris*, rooted in the margin and spreading towards the water ; a very clean-looking plant with its solid leaves and ivory-white flowers. Its near relative and natural associate, *Orontium*, may well be with it, rising from the bottom in water about a foot deep.

In the green space of rough grass between the marsh pools and the running water, there is already a fair quantity of the pretty pink-flowered Marsh Rattle (*Pedicularis*), and in the same region *Gentiana Pneumonanthe* has been planted. There is no occasion to cram this space with plants, and yet it is pleasant to come across surprises ; here and there a clump of some good Fern, or, in the drier places, some interesting Bramble.

Here also the double form of the native Lady's-smock (*Cardamine pratensis*) would be perfectly well-placed.

The lower part of the little valley (the Marsh Marigold and Alder region is at the upper) is less peaty; in parts more of an alluvial loam. Here the English Fritillaries are at home in scattered groups, some purple and some white; here also will be representatives of the small Trumpet Daffodils, *N. Pseudo-narcissus*, *N. nanus*, and *N. minor;* and here will be the Globe-flowers (*Trollius*) and the handsome purple, blue-flowered *Geranium pratense.*

PLANTS FOR THE STREAM AND STREAM-SIDE

Myosotis palustris.
Spiræa palmata.
S. Aruncus.
Iris lævigata.
Mimulus luteus.
Ranunculus aquatilis.
Lysimachia vulgaris.
Heracleum giganteum.
H. mantegazzianum.

Spiræa Ulmaria fl. pl.
S. venusta.
Osmunda regalis.
Asplenium Filix-fœmina.
Impatiens Noli-me-tangere.
Iris Pseud-acorus.
Lythrum Salicaria roseum.
Petasites vulgaris.
Caltha palustris.

PLANTS AND FERNS FOR DAMP PEATY BANK

Linnæa borealis.
Trientalis europæa.
Dryas octopetala.
Gaultheria procumbens.
G. Shallon.
Asplenium Filix-fœmina.
Nephrodium dilatatum.

Pyrola minor.
P. arenaria.
Epigæa repens.
Goodyera repens.
Mitchella repens.
Lomaria Spicant.
Osmunda regalis.

PLANTS FOR PEATY BOG-POOLS AND BEDS OF SPHAGNUM

Cypripedium spectabile.
Calla palustris.
Parnassia palustris.
Anagallis tenella.
Sibthorpia europæa.
Liparis Loeselii.
Eriophorum angustifolium.

Sarracenia purpurea.
Orontium aquaticum.
Pinguicula grandiflora.
Campanula hederacea.
Malaxis paludosa.
Narthecium ossifragum.
Drosera rotundifolia.

IN COOL PEAT

Xerophyllum asphodeloides.

Galax aphylla.

IN DAMP GRASS NEAR STREAM

Pedicularis palustris.
Fritillaria Meleagris.
Geranium pratense.
Narcissus nanus.
Cardamine pratensis, fl. pl.

Gentiana Pneumonanthe.
Trollius europæus.
Narcissus Pseudo-narcissus
N. minor.

THE GRASS OF PARNASSUS (PARNASSIA PALUSTRIS).

(See page 158.)

CHAPTER XI

A CONVERTED DITCH AND A WILD STREAM-GARDEN

BEFORE passing on to the rock-garden, that will follow, after some suitable intermediate planting, from the bog pools, it will be useful to consider what may be done when there is no pleasant, shallow stream, but only, as often occurs, a deep ditch with nearly vertical sides and a little running water at the bottom. Nothing can be less inspiring to the planter than such a ditch; yet, on the other hand, nothing is more stimulating to his power of invention, and determination to convert unsightliness into beauty. The ditch, as it exists, is useless except as a drain, but there is the precious running water—the one thing most wanted. In such a case it is often advisable to make an entirely new channel, excavating a good width so as to gain plenty of space down at the water's edge, and to give the stream some other form than a straight one. A natural stream is seldom straight, and though in gardening in general straight lines have great value, yet there are often reasons for departing from them, especially in ground-work of the wilder sort. So with our stream and its accompanying path, the character of the environment must be considered, the general lie of the land, the

167

nature of the places where the water enters and
leaves the garden, and so on. The path should swing
along in one easy line, not straight, but not going
out of its way to twist for no reason—an unpardon-
able offence in all gardening. The course of the

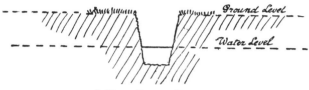

A DEEP DITCH: SECTION

stream may be more erratic, and a glance at the
sketch will show how such planning gives opportunities for planting and enjoying a limited number
of pretty things at a time, for each bend of the brook
may show quite different treatment.

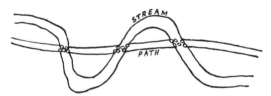

PLAN OF PATH AND ALTERED STREAM

The soil is taken out not only for the wider, shallower stream, but nearly down to the water-level
for a width of some feet on the path side. The spare
earth is thrown up beyond the path and shaped so
that it rises first gently and then a little more sharply.

The rest of the excavation goes on the other side of the stream, rising easily from rather near the water's edge. In the section the shrubs on the banks are shown of the size they would be about a year after planting ; eventually they would be quite as big again. The course of the stream is dug out less than

SECTION

A CONVERTED DITCH SHOWN IN SECTION

1 ft. deep, flattish rough stones are laid at the bottom, and over them smaller stones. If, as is likely, the path is inclined to be damp, it can be made dry and solid by ramming small stones into its surface, or it can be roughly laid with flat stones in the wettest places. The path must have the character of a wild path, not that of a garden walk—nothing that suggests rolled gravel, and no straightly-trimmed edges. The planting will be of the same character as that which has been just described and advised for the stream-garden.

Occasionally there are places where the natural conditions are all that is most inviting for the making of a stream-garden. Where these are found, and where there is a master-mind to direct, the most beautiful result may be expected. Such a happy combination occurred in the estate of Mr. H. Avray Tipping, at Mounton, Monmouthshire, whose water-garden is thus described in his own words :—

"We are convinced that when hill and rock and rushing stream arrest attention by their prominence, they should be accepted as the chief lines of a layout, that artifice should follow in their train and not oppose them, that man should, in such surroundings, leave the compass and the spirit-level and study Nature's own modes of expression. That has been the attempt at Mounton, and the results are to be judged by the accompanying illustrations. The site was a rocky limestone gorge, with sheer cliffs alternating with steep tree-clad hangers. At their foot a stream wound its way, sometimes surging round a bluff, at others running easily in the midst of a narrow meadow composed of the sandy soil brought there by the water's action of a million years. Here lay a tiny village—a parish of five hundred acres, with a population of fifty. The latter had at one time been larger, for the water-power of the stream and the oak bark of the woods had encouraged the making of packing-paper. Modern methods of free trade and large production had brought this local industry to an end, and mills and houses were fallen in or decayed; there were some cottages in sordid condition, and only a tiny church has been re-edified.

"As one or two of such cottages stood close to that part of the proposed grounds which was to become the water-garden, they had to be got hold of as opportunity offered, and so treated that they might

harmonise and add point to the general composition.
Two of them were shown in illustrations, and their
renovation was described in *Country Life* on March
21st, 1908. The general scheme of the grounds
comprised a high and airy tableland, which could
adequately accommodate on its comparatively flat
surface a house and its terraces. The latter were to
be separated by some broken rocky ground set with
heaths and low shrubs from the wooded slopes and
precipitous sides of the limestone formation, which
offered great scope for picturesque wild gardens.
Pathways were engineered along the sides of these
slopes, and they lead to the level bed of the stream
and to what was a little meadow that lay between
it and the lane. There was no hurry whatever to
realise all this scheme. It was begun ten years ago,
and the house and much of the formal lay-out on
the upper flat still remain unaccomplished. The
owner lives in the next parish, and this is the work
of his leisure moments and for the employment of
available labour in the winter months. The present
purpose is not to describe the whole grounds, but
only the water-garden, made out of the stream itself,
with the meadow on one side of it and the edge
of the slope on the other. It was at first proposed
to use the original stream-bed and its banks for
gardening purposes; but when, after some very
heavy rains, much of the new planted stuff was
swept away down-stream to Severn Sea, and when
at the close of a dry summer that which had not
been swept away in the winter suffered severely

from drought, owing to the stream becoming a mere rill, it was realised that serious alteration of the stream was necessary and that an artificial stream-bed where the water would be under command was essential.

" It is not easy to get the ordinary gardener or labourer to understand natural forms. He can dig you a ditch or a canal, or even serpentine you a walk. But they will be set out with great precision by means of pegs and a garden-line. The making of the new stream-bed therefore needed close super-vision and even the direct labour of the designer. Just before the original stream-bed took a decided turn from east to south he ordered a trench to be dug about twelve feet wide and five feet deep. This lay in the meadow, started within a few feet of the stream bank, and rejoined the original stream some eighty yards lower down. The top soil was wheeled well away, in order that it might not be buried but be replaced as the top soil in the new arrangement. The under soil was tossed on either bank as unevenly as possible. All this preliminary work could be carried out by the labourers alone, but that done, the constant attention of the designer was essential. Uneven side bays were dug out on each side of the trench, while portions of the heaped soil were raked back into it. The accidental unevennesses produced by this process were used as a basis for establishing curves, levels and contours as closely as possible resembling those of Nature. At the bottom of the trench a small water-way was engineered, its wind-

"Occasionally there are places where the natural conditions are all that is most inviting for the making of a stream-garden. Where these are found, and where there is a master-mind to direct, the most beautiful result may be expected."

ings being made reasonable by the introduction of realistic bluffs, and the differing widths being made ₊convincing by the placing of barrier rocks. The same system makes all the zigzags and ups and downs of the pathways reasonable, the paths themselves being mostly laid with rough limestone paving procured from a stratum in a neighbouring quarry, which works out into slabs two or three inches thick and with fairly flat surfaces. The water was let in from the natural to the artificial stream-bed through a pipe in the bank, which can be closed, half opened or fully opened at will. The water is made to look, at its entry, as if it bubbled up amid great stones from a spring. It then dances rapidly down over stones and round corners until it reaches a wider and more level portion of the bed, where it lies placidly, and is crossed by the stepping-stones that form the foreground of one of the pictures. Reference to page 180 shows the wider original stream appearing first on the left-hand side of the plan, crossing its top and then turning downwards. The narrow artificial stream lies within this curve. The scheme of the pathways looks eccentric and ridiculous on the flat sheet of paper, but it is the result of strict causation and nowhere offends the eye. There are considerable areas of much broken and often rocky ground encompassing both stream-beds, all of which is planted. Away from streams or paths flowering shrubs of some size are set. Lilacs, Japanese Guelder Roses, Judas-trees, Weigelas, Deutzias and Philadelphus represent the deciduous section, while for

THE STEPPING-STONES.

THE PLANTED STREAM-SIDE.

evergreens we find Choisyas and Savins. Tall perennials group with these or stretch out beyond them,
such as Rudbeckia laciniata, Anemone japonica and
Phloxes. Lower growths at first intermingle and
then dominate as the path is approached. Lavender
bushes, prostrate Junipers and Cotoneaster horizontalis
are associated with Harebells, Foam-flower, dwarf
Irises, Stonecrops and their like. The stream edge
is set with water-loving plants. The great leaves of
Saxifraga peltata and Rodgersia podophylla give horizontal lines, while New Zealand Flax and Siberian
Irises soar aloft.

"The whole race of Astilbes flourishes amazingly
and reproduces itself by seed. This planted ground
has taken up half the width of what was meadow,
but the other half is used as lawn. Next to the road
there are a wall, a shrubbery border and a path. The
open shed that served for the animals that pastured
in the meadow is used as a tool-house, but its eaves
are brought forward so as to afford a sheltered and
covered seat, from which the water-garden and the
great cliff can be enjoyed by the eye. The lawn
itself is no longer level like the meadow was, but
presents the appearance of an unused stream-bed
grassed over. The effect is very satisfactory, but the
plan was adopted for purely practical reasons. The
occasional torrential rains of this Welsh borderland
bring down such masses of water that injurious floods
occur. Their destructive action can only be obviated
by getting rid of the water as quickly as possible.
The sharp bend of the old stream tends to hold it

back, and so a flood-gate is introduced at the head
of the lawn, and when much pressure of water
threatens it is opened, and a great part of the water
pours down the centre of the lawn, obviating all
danger to the garden and to the low-lying gardener's
cottage.

"Despite its vagaries of water-level, a good deal of
gardening, prudently ordained, takes place on the
banks of the old stream. Portions of them are kept
high above flood-level, other portions have been cut
low, but are arranged in the manner of bays between
bluffs, so that though they may be flooded there is
no uprooting rush of water. As regards planting,
where the spot is exposed care is taken to introduce
strong-rooting subjects only. By this means the
occasional spates are no longer destructive and the
subsidence of the water leaves matters as they were.
More delicate planting of water subjects takes place
along the sides of the artificial stream. Here one
of the greatest successes is Primula rosea. This
Himalayan variety, while by no means so particular
and miffy as others of the family, is not everywhere
at home. Here it not only grows luxuriantly, but
sows itself freely, and considerable stretches of
damp ground on either side of the stepping-stones
are studded by myriads of bright pink blooms in
March. The water-garden continues for some way
beyond the limits of the plan, the little village
church, grouping in with the gardener's cottage and
the largest of the bridges, gives an architectural
character to its lower end. But the lofty cliff and

THE ARTIFICIAL STREAM AND A PAVED PATH.

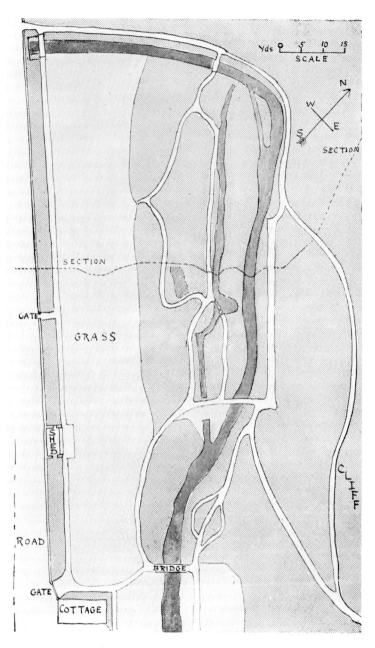

PLAN OF PART OF THE STREAM-GARDEN AT MOUNTON.

the tall trees, as well as the rushing water and luxuriant plant-life, make Nature the predominant partner in this rural retreat.   She rules supreme, and art is but a humble handmaid who seeks to still her passions, curb her wildness and give added value to her beauties."

CHAPTER XII

THE ROCK-GARDEN—GENERAL ARRANGEMENT

AFTER the marsh pools described in Chapter X., and still on the homeward journey, and between this region and the shrubbery portion of the garden proper, will be the rock-garden (see plan, p119),approached on the marsh side by some of the plants of rather large size. Nothing is more strikingly beautiful than a large patch of *Equisetum Telmateia,* a native plant ; mysterious, graceful, and almost tropical-looking. Near it there are two large-leaved plants, *Saxifraga peltata,* in moist rich soil carrying its great leaves three feet high, and *Rodgersia podophylla,* with palmate leaves as large as those of the Horse Chestnut, but the divisions handsomely jagged at the ends, and the whole leaf of a fine reddish-bronze colouring. It is sometimes crippled by late frosts, and well deserves the protection of a few Fir boughs.

If there is space enough here would also be a place for the giant Gunneras (besides their other water-side sites), and for another spreading patch of *Heracleum mantegazzianum,* for *Arundo Donax,* and for the Bamboos. These giant Reeds and Grasses should in such a good garden as this have a large space, of which they would be the chief occupants. They should be

IN A FINE ROCK GARDEN.

ZENOBIA (ANDROMEDA) SPECIOSA (FULL SIZE).
Type of small evergreen flowering shrub for the Rock-Garden.

in bold, informal clumps, with easy grassy ways pass
ing between. In the present case the fringe of their
masses on the rock-garden side is approached by
shrubs that will enjoy the same conditions. These
will be Kalmias, Azaleas, Ledums, Andromedas, Vacciniums, Gaultherias, and Myricas, the bog and peat-
loving shrubs. Of these the Kalmias and Myricas will
suit the dampest places. As clumps or groups of
these approach the rock-garden they will join on to
it without any jarring obstruction. The green path
that skirts the cool foot of the mound or promontory
that forms the rock-garden will only be one of
several others that pass among the Bamboos and join
the path that we came along by the bog pools. The
plan shows the general arrangement. Even where the
peaty foot of the rock-mound comes down to the
level, the rock-garden's influence will still cross the
grass path; for the same kind of planting is continued
on the other side, only then dying away into the larger
growths that will continue the scheme of planting in
that direction.

Now we are clear of the Fir-wood hill, and the
ground to the south-west, though still slightly rising,
and thinly wooded with Oak, Thorn, and Holly, is not
steep enough to shade the rock-garden; moreover, some
trees have been cut away to insure that full light and
clear air space that so many rock-plants need.

The rock-garden has been made in what was a
natural knoll of sharply rising ground, or rather a
kind of promontory thrust out from the wood.

Three main paths pass through it; the one on the right skirts the natural foot of the promontory, passing first north-east, then north, then a little north-west; the one to the left mounts its shoulder by an easy ascent, partly excavated so as to give rocky banks right and left; but it is nearly level at the top before coming to the further descent. Here will be the place for fine short turf to be pierced by the bloom of mountain bulbs, Snowdrops, Spring Snowflakes, and the like; each kind having its own little region, informally bordered by some group of small bushes.

The third path will be cut through the heart of the knoll, gently turning, and having steep banks right and left. In forming such a rock-garden as this the rock-builder must use all his skill, so that the lines of the work shall not only be good in themselves, but shall not jar with anything that comes before or after, or with any view of the half distance that can be seen from any portion of the garden scheme.

This scheme of three main pathways supposes a fair space of ground, such as a third of an acre to half an acre. If less space has to be dealt with it is better to have an easy path alone and a sloping bank on either side, as in the good rock-garden shown in the illustration on p.188.

When the ground is shaped and the rocks placed, the next matter of importance, and that will decide whether the rock-garden is to be a thing of some dignity or only the usual rather fussy mixture, is to have a solid planting of suitable small shrubs crowning all the heights. Most important of these will

STEPS IN ROCK-GARDEN, AS IN PLAN BETWEEN N AND B.

A WELL-ARRANGED ROCK-GARDEN IN THE FORM OF A LITTLE
VALLEY.

be the Alpine Rhododendrons; neat in habit, dark
of foliage, and on a scale that does not overwhelm
the little plant jewels that are to come near them.
No shrubs are so suitable for a good part of the main
plantings in the higher regions. Then there will be
Heaths, among which the white *Menziesia* would be
largely used on the cooler exposures, and Pernettyas
in quantity. The pretty and fragrant *Ledum palustre*
will also be a useful shrub in the backward regions of
the cooler portions, while the neat *L. buxifolium*, on
the fringes of the solid shrub planting, will lead well to
the smaller plants. Other shrubs that will suit these
upper portions are *Cistus laurifolius*, *Cistus cyprius*,
with Spanish Gorse and various Brooms in the hottest places; Andromedas, Gaultherias, Pernettyas, and
Ledums will come in the cooler spots. In addition
to the Alpine Rhododendrons there will be *R. myrtifolium* and several small garden hybrids.

These are all shrubs of dark coloured foliage; by
using them in bold masses they will give the whole
rock-garden that feeling of unity and simplicity
of design that often in such places is so painfully
wanting.

Other small evergreen shrubs, such as Skimmias
and *Daphne pontica* should also be used rather near
together, but from their brighter and paler colour
preferably in a group by themselves.

By working on such a general plan we shall avoid
that rude shock so often experienced when the rock-
garden comes into view, from its appearance being
so uncompromisingly sudden. Perhaps there is a

smooth bit of lawn, with pleasant easy lines of flower or shrub clump; then you pass round some bush, and all at once there is a shockingly *sudden* rock-garden. I cannot think of any other term that gives the impression I wish to convey. It often comes of want of space. Only a certain space can be given to the rock-plants, and it must be made the most of; still, even in small gardens it might be more or less prepared or led up to. But I am not just now considering the limitations of the smallest gardens (a tempting theme, but one that should be taken by itself), but rather the best way to lay out ground that is neither cramped in space nor stinted of reasonable labour. Therefore, where the region of groups of handsome hardy moisture-loving exotics ends (to the left of M and P on the plan), we come to an occasional flattish boulder or blunt-nosed rock just rising above the ground, as the path rises very gently. Presently these large plants, of which the furthest back were in quite moist ground, are left behind, and we are among bushes four to seven feet high (N and above on plan). These give place to lower shrubs, rather more thinly grouped, while the rocky boulders are more frequent and more conspicuous. Presently, and only by a gentle transition, the rock-mound comes into view, and we see that there are three paths, each having a slightly different aspect, while the whole mound, clothed with dark, close-growing, and for the most part, dwarf shrubs, has a unity of character which presents no shock to the mind, but only a pleasant invitation to come

PATH IN ROCK-GARDEN.

"*It can never be repeated too often that in this* [*the rock garden*] *as in all kinds of gardening where some kind of beauty is aimed at, the very best effects are made by the simplest means, and by the use of a few different kinds of plants only at a time.*"

and see and enjoy. There is no bewilderment, because there is no jumble or crowding of irrelevant items. Everything falls into its place, and a quiet progress through any one of the paths presents a succession of garden-pictures that look not so much as if they had been designed and made but as if they had just happened to come so. There is nothing perhaps to provoke that violent excitement of wonderment so dear to the uneducated, but there will be, alike to the plant lover and to the garden artist, the satisfaction of a piece of happy gardening, without strain or affectation, beautiful and delightful in all its parts and growing easily and pleasantly out of its environment.

The shrubs named as those best fitted for the upper portions of the rock may well have an occasional exception, for though the masses must be large enough to give a feeling of dignity, they must not degenerate into monotony. This can be secured either by the free growth or rather overgrowth of some of the shrubs named, such as that of Brooms and *Cistus cyprius* or by the use of a shrub of larger stature, such as Juniper.

Veronica Traversi, as it grows older and assumes a small tree shape, is one of this class and *Cassinia fulvida* is another. Rosemary and Lavender also, after a few years of rather close and neat growth, rise and spread and open out, showing trunk-like stems. This older state, which has a somewhat unkempt look in the neater parts of the garden, give these shrubs that rather wilder habit that fits them all the better for their place among the boulders of the rocky heights.

There is also a class of shrub of trailing character that is most useful for leading from those of stiffer growth on the higher ground, to the lower regions where there will be more flowery plants. The low growing Cotoneasters, Savin, and *Mühlenbeckia*, are some of the best of these, and Heaths of many kinds from the tall Tree Heath of the Mediterranean to the low-growing and early-blooming *Erica carnea*. Among the different kinds of Heath nothing can well exceed the usefulness of the white *Menziesia*, for it is not only a neat dark green tuft in winter, but in all the summer months and even into autumn it bears its large Heath-bells in good quantity.

These dwarf shrubs should be planted so as to appear to stream out of the dark and solid growths above, following and accentuating the stratified lines in which the stones are laid. If they are planted just above the stones they will fall naturally into their places.

It will also add greatly to the feeling of general cohesion which it is so important to obtain in such a garden, if below these again the same kind of scheme is carried out in plants that have some kind of solidity of appearance or persistence throughout the year, such as Thrift and *Asarum;* their long-enduring dark foliage being highly becoming as a setting to flowers of lively colour. Ferns also, on the shady side, should be used in the same way, while on the sunniest exposures the same idea would be carried out by some of the

HYBRID ROCK PINKS.

A LARGE PLANTING OF THRIFT, WITH VIOLA FLORIARENSIS.

neat whitish or glaucous-leaved plants, Rock Pinks, *Antennaria, Achillea,* and so on.

Now and then among the small shrubs, and just below the larger ones, a single plant of bold aspect will make a great effect, though the general scheme of planting should be in easy informal groups or long drifts. The kind of plant to use in these points of exceptional isolation is such a one as the best type of *Eryngium alpinum,* or one of the more important Euphorbias, or a tuft of *Yucca flaccida.*

If the rock-garden is very large, larger than the one in contemplation, great groups of the nobler Yuccas are magnificent, but they would be on a scale rather too large for the present garden.

EVERGREEN SHRUBS FOR THE UPPER PART OF THE
ROCK-GARDEN

Rhododendron ferrugineum.
R. hirsutum.
R. myrtifolium.
Pernettya, vars.
Abies clanbraziliana.
A. pumila.
Juniperus Sabina.
Lavender.
Rosemary.
Erica carnea.
E. Tetralix alba.
E. arborea.
E. ciliaris, E. vagans.
E. cinerea, vars.
Calluna, vars.
Menziesia polifolia.
Mühlenbeckia complexa.

Cotoneaster horizontalis.
C. microphylla.
Cassinia fulvida.
Double Gorse.
Genista præcox.
G. andreana.
Cistus laurifolius.
C. cyprius.
Ruscus racemosus.
Veronica Traversi.
Daphne Mezereum.
D. pontica.
D. Cneorum.
Genista hispania.
Andromeda floribunda.
A. Catesbæi.
Zenobia speciosa.

PLAN OF THE ROCK-GARDEN AND GROUND SURROUNDING IT

The dark tinting shows the dwarf shrubs on the rock-garden and in the portions or clumps connected with it.

At the top of the plan is wooded ground, mostly of oak and holly, gradually rising out of the top of the plan. It sinks a little right and left, chiefly to the left where an arrow shows the direction of drainage into the last of the bog-pools in a sort of shallow sub-valley between the oak-wooded ground and the fir-wooded hill. This hill is out of the plan to the left top.

A, B, C, D, shows the line of the ridge of the knoll on which the rock-garden is made, D being the lowest point where the foot of the knoll dies away into the level.

The portion described as of high shrubs leading to the rock-garden is shown at N and above it, across the path, the uppermost of the three rock-garden paths.

Leading up the steps to B is the portion laid in granite, C in limestone, D in sand and peat.

H is a clump which on one side feels the influence of the rock-garden, while the other side, next the wider grass paths, belongs to the clump I.

H is planted at the top end with small shrubs in relation to the rock-garden end above it, as is also the tip of O and the right hand end of N. The large groups marked in M, O, P, J, and I are important plantings of Bamboos. The smaller plants among these in the same groups and also in H are for the most part hardy Azaleas, with Kalmias and some of the larger of the Vacciniums and Andromerias. In N the Kalmias are indicated by a half-dark tint, the lighter circular forms standing for Azaleas. There are also some Azaleas in H and a few in I, but the circles in I that measure twelve to fifteen feet across are free-growing Roses.

Between P and J the greater number of the Azaleas are the large hardy yellow *A. pontica*. At M, and just right and left, which is a cool bank, almost wet towards the path, are clumps of plants of large foliage and important aspect, such as *Gunnera* and *Arunda Donax*.

K and L show groups of Birch trees accompanied by Holly, and from L towards A and E are large bushes of Holly with Oaks.

Between L and B, backing the smaller bushes tinted dark, are clumps of Juniper, which occur again on the bank beyond G towards F and E. At E and between K and L are paths leading into woodland ; not garden paths but wood paths.

The large grass paths leading out of the plan to the right go towards the home garden and the house.

To the right of J and I (out of the plan) is the place for a good plantation of Rhododendrons, out of sight of the Azaleas and hidden from them by the large group of Bamboos.

In the region of A, E, and F would be long drifts of Daffodils ; here also white Foxgloves would be sown.

PLAN OF THE ROCK-GARDEN AND ITS NEIGHBOURHOOD.

CERASTIUM IN DRY WALL.

SOME OF THE EASIEST GROWN ROCK-GARDEN PLANTS.

Acæna microphylla, pulchella.
Achillea umbellata.
Adonis vernalis.
Æthionema grandiflorum.
Ajuga, vars.
Alchemilla alpina.
Alyssum saxatile.
Anemone blanda, nemorosa,
    vars., *sylvestris, apennina.*
Anthericum Liliastrum, Liliago.
Antennaria dioica, tomentosa.
Antirrhinum glutinosum.
Arabis albida, and double var.
Arenaria balearica, montana.
Armeria vulgaris, Cephalotes.
Artemisia sericea.
Asarum europæum.
Aster alpinus.
Aubrietia deltoides, græca.
Campanula pulla, cæspitosa,
    carpatica, pusilla, barbata.
Cardamine pratensis fl. pl., tri-
    folia.
Cerastium tomentosum.
Coptis trifolia.
Cheiranthus alpinus, Mar-
    shalli.
Corydalis bulbosa, capnoides.
Delphinium nudicaule.
Dentaria diphylla.
Dianthus cæsius, deltoides, fra-
    grans, and vars.
Draba aizoides.
Epimedium macranthum.
Erica, vars.
Erinus alpinus.

Gentiana acaulis, asclepiadea.
Helianthemum, vars.
Hemerocallis Dumortieri.
Hieracium aurantiacum, villo-
    sum.
Hutchinsia alpina.
Iberis sempervirens.
Iris cristata, pumila, vars.
Linaria alpina, pallida, hepati-
    cæfolia.
Linum flavum.
Lithospermum prostratum.
Lychnis alpina
Mentha Requieni.
Mimulus cupreus.
Nierembergia rivularis.
Orobus vernus, aurantius.
Papaver alpinum.
Phlox setacea, vars.
Polygala Chamæbuxus.
Polygonum affine, vaccini-
    folium.
Potentilla alchemilloides
    dubia.
Primula rosea, denticulata,
    sikkimensis.
Sanguinaria canadensis.
Saponaria ocymoides.
Saxifraga, Sempervivum, **and**
    Sedum, many sps.
Silene alpestris.
Thymus lanuginosus, Serpyl-
    lum albus.
Tiarella cordifolia.
Uvularia grandiflora.
Vesicaria utriculata.

*ÆTHIONEMA, ALYSSUM, AND ROCK CAMPANULAS;
WHITE CRANESBILL BELOW.*

HELIANTHEMUM FORMOSUM AT A ROCK-FOOT.

CHAPTER XIII

THE ROCK-GARDEN (*continued*)

IT can never be repeated too often that in this, as in all kinds of gardening where some kind of beauty is aimed at, the very best effects are made by the simplest means, and by the use of a few different kinds of plants only at a time. A confused and crowded composition is a fault in any picture ; in the pictures that we paint with living plants just as much as in those that are drawn and painted on paper or canvas. Moreover, the jumbled crowd of incongruous items, placed without thought of their effect on one another, can only make a piece of chance patchwork ; it can never make a design. However interesting the individual plants may be, we want to get good proportion and beautiful combination in order to make the good garden-picture, while the individuals themselves gain in importance by being shown at their best. I have therefore thought it would be helpful to put together lists of plants for the different situations, and within the lists to bracket the names of some that look the best as near neighbours. In many cases they can be intergrouped at the edges. These lists appear at the end of the chapter. Where the same plant is named more than once, it is to be understood that it is good

AUBRIETIA IN THE ROCK-GARDEN.

LITHOSPERMUM PROSTRATUM (BRIGHT BLUE) HANGING OVER ROCK ; A SILVERY SAXIFRAGE BELOW.

to use in more than one combination. A few examples
of such groupings of plants will be described, and
others given in the lists.

When I think of the rock-garden plants, and try to
bring to mind those that have given me most pleasure
for a fair length of time, I think the roll of honour
must begin with *Lithospermum prostratum.* There are
many that give one as keen a feeling of delight and
thankfulness for a week or ten days, or even a little
more ; but for steady continuance of beautiful bloom
I can think of nothing so full of merit. It is, therefore, the best of plants for any important rocky knoll,
and, as its habit is to trail downwards, it may well go
on the very top of some jutting promontory fairly to
the front, or be at the top of a bit of almost wall-like
rock-work as in the picture. It is neat-looking all the
year through, and the deep colour of the small rough
leaves sets off the strong pure blue of the flowers. In
winter the leaves turn to a kind of black bronze, but
never lose their neat appearance, as of a well-fitting
ground carpet. The colour blue in the garden, as also
in other fields of decorative practice, seems to demand
a treatment by contrast as an exception to the generally
desirable rule of treatment by harmony. Therefore I
do not hesitate to plant near the *Lithospermum* the
brilliant pale yellow *Cheiranthus alpinus,* and, though
I do not find use for many plants with variegated
foliage, I like to have in the same group the pretty
little *Arabis lucida variegata.*

Among a host of plants that are of so eminent a
degree of merit that it is almost impossible to give

precedence to any one, *Achillea umbellata* takes high rank. The two illustrations in the chapter on the Sunny Rock-wall (pp. 26, 29) show it both in summer bloom and winter foliage. With this charming thing I should group some of the plants of low-toned pink blossom, such as Thrift and the pink-flowered Cudweed (*Antennaria*), and any of the encrusted Saxifrages; or separately with the charming *Phlox setacea* "Vivid," in this case with nothing else then in bloom quite near.

There are some little plants that grow in sheets, whose bloom is charming, but on so small a scale that other flowers of larger size or stouter build would seem to crush them. Such a one is the dainty little Linnæa, which should have a cool shady region of its own among tiny Ferns, and nothing large to overmaster it.

The little creeping *Linaria hepaticæfolia* is another of this small, dainty class, best accompanied by things of a like stature, such as *Arenaria balearica*, and perhaps little Ferns and Mossy Saxifrages. *Arenaria balearica* is a little gem for any cool rocky place; it grows fast and clings close to the stones. It always spreads outwardly, seeking fresh pasture; after a time dying away in the middle. The illustration having this *Arenaria* on the angle of a small rock-garden shows a little dark patch on its surface, first flowerless and then dying away, while the outer fringe of the patch grows onward. *Aubrietia, Arabis, Iberis,* and *Cerastium,* four of the commonest of spring-blooming plants of Alpine origin that have long been grown in

ARENARIA BALEARICA (AT THE ANGLE AND ON PATH), AND DOUBLE CUCKOO-FLOWER
IN A SMALL ROCK-GARDEN.

*BOLD PLANTING CARRIED OUT WITH GREAT EFFECT IN THE
ROCK GARDEN.*

gardens, are capital companions, making sheets of
hanging or trailing bloom at that flowery time when
spring joins hands with summer. The palest coloured
of the Aubrietias, such as the variety " Lavender,"
are among the best, and should not be neglected
in favour of the stronger purples only.

A little later in the year *Campanula pulla* and *Silene
alpestris* do well together, plentifully framed with
small Ferns and Mossy Saxifrages. The lovely *Iris
cristata* is charming with *Corydalis ochroleuca* of the
pale yellowish-white bloom and bluish almost feathery
leaves.

In the upper and bolder regions of the rock-
garden where there will be small shrubs, the fine
blue-flowered dwarf Flag Iris, *I. Cengialti*, should
be grouped under a bush of *Eurybia gunniana*.

London Pride, the best of the Saxifrages of that
class, should be plentifully grouped with strong
patches of the lovely white St. Bruno's Lily, backed
by some bushes of dark foliage as of *Gaultheria
Shallon* or Alpine Rhododendron.

It is one of the pleasures of the rock-garden to
observe what plants (blooming at the same time) will
serve to make these pretty mixtures, and to see how
to group and arrange them (always preferably in
long-shaped drifts) in such a way that they will best
display their own and each other's beauty ; so that
a journey through the garden, while it presents
a well-balanced and dignified harmony throughout its
main features and masses, may yet at every few steps
show a succession of charming lesser pictures.

It is only possible to point to a few examples, but those who work carefully in their rock-gardens will see the great gain that rewards a little care and thought in putting the right things together. If they will take the trouble to work out the few examples given, they will be able to invent many other such combinations for themselves.

Then there comes the question of putting the right plants in the right places. The hybrid Rock Pinks, derived from several alpine species, and our native Dianthus cæsius, are among the best and the happiest of rock plants. They revel in light and sunshine and seem to enjoy adaptation of growth to the conditions that may be presented; forming dense, close cushions on rocky levels, and deeply-draping sheets of leaf and bloom where they find an invitation to hang down the rocky face.

Where the garden adjoins ground of a rocky, or rocky and woody character, the difficulty of construction is reduced to the lowest point. There are thousands of acres of such ground in the remoter parts of our islands, many of them no doubt so placed that with a very little alteration and the addition of just the right plants, the most beautiful of rock-gardens could be made. Such ground as a rocky wood with its own Foxgloves such as sometimes occurs could hardly be bettered as a rock-garden background, and would suggest bold treatment, indeed would absolutely forbid anything petty or niggling.

It is highly interesting to have a space in one of the warmest and most sheltered regions of the rock-

SMALL HYBRID PINKS.

HARDY RED-FLOWERED OPUNTIA (O. XANTHOSTEMA) IN
STEEP ROCK-WORK.

garden for the hardy Opuntias. They are the more desirable in that they are not only the sole representatives of the large Cactus family that are hardy in England, but that they are also desirable flowering plants, of large bloom and moderate habit of growth. The family comprises so many species of monstrously ungainly or otherwise unsightly form that it is fortunate for our gardens that the hardy species should be beautiful things.

Opuntia Raffinesquii has long been with us, and more lately we have had the good yellow-bloomed species *O. camanchica, arenaria, fragilis,* and *Engelmanni.* To these with yellow flowers have been added still later *O. rhodanthe* and *O. xanthostema.* They are all North American plants, most of them natives of Colorado. They like a place among steep rocks in a soil of poor sand and broken limestone, in the hottest exposure. The only thing they dislike in our climate is long-continued rain, from which the steep rock-wall in a great measure protects them, by means of the complete drainage that it secures.

We have a fine example of good rock-gardening accessible to the public in the Royal Gardens, Kew. Here there is not only a copious collection of mountain plants of the kinds suitable for rock-gardens and their immediate neighbourhood, but we see them as well arranged as is possible in an establishment that, it must be remembered, is primarily botanical; indeed the way in which the gardens have been of late years enriched with large breadths of bulbous plants in grass and beautiful flowering shrubs, not in single specimens only, but in bold groups, has been a powerful means of instruction, and has done as much as anything to help people to know the good plants and how best to use them.

Of private gardens one of the most remarkable is that at Friar Park, near Henley-on-Thames, designed and personally arranged by Sir Frank Crisp ; over ten thousand tons of rock having gone to its making. One cannot do better than quote the words of Mr. Correvon in his admirable book, *Flore Alpine:* "What constitutes its beauty is the harmony of the lines, and above all the dimensions of the plants with regard to the rocks ; a combination of qualities presenting to the eye a comprehensive view of excellent proportion. It is all true to scale, a point rarely observed in the making of rock-gardens. Plants of large size and broad foliage are grouped at the base ; while through successive rising levels one passes to the absolutely dwarf and close-growing flowers of the heights."

In planting the rock-garden it is a good plan to allot fairly long stretches of space to nearly related and nearly allied plants, especially to those genera that contain many desirable species and varieties. Several genera will be largely represented ; of these the principal are *Saxifraga, Sedum, Sempervivum, Campanula, Silene, Linaria, Iberis, Iris, Draba, Dianthus,* and *Primula.* This way of grouping, if well arranged with some intergrouping of smaller plants, will not only have the best effect but will have a distinct botanical interest ; not botanical in the drier sense of

A BANK OF SPRING-FLOWERING ALPINE PLANTS
(ARABIS, AUBRIETIA, ETC.).

RILL AND POOL IN ROCK-GARDEN.

mere classification, but botanical as a living exposition of variation of form within the law of a common structure.

Besides the grouping in families, the following list contains, bracketed together, names of plants that have a good effect when grouped near each other :—

{ *Lithospermum prostratum.*
Cheiranthus alpinus.
Arabis lucida variegata.

{ *Achillea umbellata.*
Antennaria tomentosa.
Armeria vulgaris.
A. Cephalotes.
Saxifraga (encrusted vars.).

{ *Linaria hepaticæfolia.*
L. pallida.
Small Ferns.

{ *Cardamine pratensis fl. pl.*
Arenaria balearica.
Mossy Saxifrage.

{ *Aubrietia græca*, &c.
Arabis albida.
Iberis sempervirens.
Cerastium tomentosum.

{ *Iberis correæfolia.*
Phacelia campanularia(sown).
Mossy Saxifrage.

{ *Cornus canadensis.*
Waldsteinea fragarioides.

{ *Adonis vernalis.*
Tulipa sylvestris.

{ *Tunica Saxifraga.*
Saponaria ocymoides.
Dianthus deltoides.

{ *Vesicaria utriculata.*
Cheiranthus mutabilis.

{ *Silene alpestris.*
Campanula pulla.

{ *Saxifraga umbrosa.*
Anthericum liliastrum.

{ *Silene maritima fl. pl.*
Othonnopsis cheirifolia.

{ *Iris cristata.*
Corydalis ochroleuca.

{ *Tiarella cordifolia.*
Myosotis dissitiflora major.
Mertensia virginica.

{ *Ramondia pyrenaica.*
Haberlea rhodopensis.
Cystopterisfragilis.

{ *Dianthus alpinus.*
Cardamine trifoliata.
Hutchinsia alpina.

{ *Achillea Clavennæ.*
Scabiosa Pterocephala.

{ *Anemone blanda.*
Galanthus Elwesi.

{ *Iris reticulata.*
Mossy Saxifrage.

{ *Orobus vernus.*
Aubrietia græca.

{ *Veronica satureifolia.*
Silene alpestris.

{ *Anemone apennina.*
Trillium grandiflorum.
Omphalodes verna.

Some Bulbous Plants for the Rock-Garden

Acis autumnalis.
Triteleia uniflora.
Crocus species.
Narcissus minor.
N. minimus.
N. Bulbocodium
N. B. citrinus.
N. juncifolius.
N. odorus minor.
N. poeticus verbanus.
N. triandrus.
Leucojum vernum.
Galanthus Elwesii.
Fritillaria armena.
F. aurea.
F. pudica.
F. Meleagris.
Oxalis enneaphylla.
Cyclamen Atkinsii and vars.
C. Coum.
C. repandum.
C. europæum.
Anomatheca cruenta.
Chionodoxa Luciliæ.
C. sardensis.
Dodecatheon, vars.
Puschkinia libanotica.
Corydalis bulbosa.
C. bracteata.
Sternbergia lutea.
Tecophilæa cyanocrocus.
Eucomis punctata.

Scilla sibirica.
S. italica alba.
S. bifolia and vars.
Muscari botryoides and white var.
M. azureum.
Tulipa Greigi.
T. persica.
T. kaufmanniana.
T. sylvestris.
Iris reticulata.
I. reticulata Krelagei.
I. Danfordiæ.
I. bakeriana.
I. balkana.
I. Cengialti.
I. olbiensis.
I. pumila and vars.
I. Chamæiris.
I. tolmeana.
Lilium croceum.
L. elegans and vars.
L. longiflorum.
L. Browni.
L. Krameri.
L. rubellum.
L. tenuifolium.
Erythronium Dens-canis, vars.
E. giganteum.
E. grandiflorum.
E. Hartwegi.
Trillium grandiflorum.
T. sessile.

Dwarf Shrubs and Half-shrubby Plants and Others of Rather Solid Habit for the Use Advised ON P. 189.

Polygala Chamæbuxus.
Polygonum vaccinifolium.
Dryas octopetala.

Cornus canadensis.
Tiarella cordifolia.
Asarum europæum.

Salix reticulata.
Andromeda tetragona.
Gaultheria procumbens.
Iberis sempervirens.
I. correæfolia.
Menziesia polifolia.
Megasea, smaller vars.

Armeria vulgaris.
A. cephalotes.
Genista saggitalis.
Daphne blagayana.
D. Cneorum.
Spiræa decumbens.
Erica carnea, and other Heaths

CHAPTER XIV

THE ALPINE GARDEN

THIS chapter is for the most part a résumé of the teaching conveyed in some highly interesting and instructive letters to *The Garden* from Mr. Henry Correvon of the gardens of Floraire, Chêne-Bourg, Geneva. No one is more intimately acquainted with the flora of the Alps than Mr. Correvon, or is better able to instruct and advise upon their use and adaptation to our gardens.

In making an Alpine garden, and considering what plants are to adorn it, it must be remembered that in the mountains of Europe there are whole chains that are of limestone and others that are entirely of granite. Many of the failures in our rock and Alpine gardens are due to this fact either being unknown or disregarded. Each of those two great main geological formations has a flora proper to itself. It stands to reason, therefore, that if we plant a shrub or herb that belongs to the granite on a calcareous soil, or a limestone plant on granite, that we are only inviting failure.

It is true that there are a good many Alpine plants that will grow in almost any soil, and a number of

SAXIFRAGA LONGIFOLIA : THE LARGEST-FLOWERED OF THE SILVERY OR ENCRUSTED SAXIFRAGES.

others that are fairly well content with one that is not their own, but there are a certain number that are not so tolerant, and if we would do the very best we can for the lovely plants of the mountain regions they should be given the kind of soil and rock that suits them best.

From its very beginning then, if an Alpine garden is to be made in a calcareous soil let it be planted with the lime-loving plants and those that are tolerant in the matter of soil, but not with those that demand granite. Hitherto the mistakes of amateurs may have been excused, because in the books and plant lists that have till now been available the great importance of this has not been clearly and concisely put before them.

If the Alpine garden is to accommodate a larger range of plants than those proper to the one soil, or if preparation from the first has to be made for plants of these two geological divisions, it is well that one distinct portion of the garden should be prepared with limestone and the other with granite. In this way it will not only be easier to work the garden and to know the destination of any newcomer, but the plants themselves will be in better harmony. I would earnestly counsel intending planters, if they have to do with a small space only, to be content with plants of the one or the other class of soil, because, as in all other kinds of gardening, the mere dotting of one plant, or of two or three only of a kind, will never make a beautiful garden, but at the best can

"In the case of a wild forest pool. . . Here is a glimpse of quiet natural beauty; pure nature untouched. . . it would be an ill deed to mar its perfection by any meddlesome gardening. The most one could do in such a place, where. . . the dragon-fly flashes in the broken midsummer light, would be to plant in the upper ground some native wild flower that would be in harmony with the place. . . but nothing that would recall the garden. Here is pure forest, and garden should not intrude. Above all, the water-margin should be left as it is."

only show a kind of living herbarium. Single examples of these lovely little children of the great mountains may be delightful things to have, and in the very smallest spaces no doubt will be all that is possible ; but we wish to consider gardening in its nobler aspects, not merely the successful cultivation of single specimens of the Alpine flora.

In planning an important Alpine garden it should be remembered that in preparing homes for some of the best of these lovely plants, not only the rocky places must be considered, but the grassy ones as well, for the pasture land of the Alps is as bright with flowers as the more rocky portions. It is here that are found the Snowflakes and the Snowdrops, the Dog-tooth Violets and the Anemones of the Pulsatilla group. Here also are the glorious *Gentiana acaulis*, the bright gem-like *G. verna*, and in boggy places *G. bavarica*, near in size to *G. verna*, and sometimes mistaken for it, but different in the shape and arrangement of its more crowded leaves, and in the still more penetrating brilliancy of its astounding blue. These little gems are not often seen at their best in English gardens, but *G. acaulis* is a much more willing colonist, and in some gardens where the soil is a rich loam it grows rapidly and flowers abundantly and proves one of the best of plants for a garden edging. Though properly a plant of the pastures, the illustration shows how kindly it takes to the rock-garden in England (p. 228).

The difficulty of imitating the close short turf of

SAXIFRAGA BURSERIANA. (One-third natural size.)

GENTIANELLA (GENTIANA ACAULIS) IN AN ENGLISH ROCK-GARDEN.

the upland Alpine pasture is that here the grasses grow too rank and tall; the only ones therefore that should be employed are the smallest of the wiry-leaved kinds, such as the short Sheep's Fescue with the tufted base.

A true Alpine garden, it should be understood, is a place where plants native to the Alps alone are grown. It should not be confused with a general rock-garden where we have mountain and other plants from the whole temperate world.

Besides those that one generally classes as plants, meaning flowering plants, there will be many of the beautiful small Ferns of the Alps to be considered, and the small shrubs whose presence is so important in the more prominent eminences of our rock-gardens and the tops of our rock-walls. Of the latter, in the true Alpine garden, the most important are the dwarf Rhododendrons, and nothing could be so fitting a groundwork or setting for the little bright-blossomed jewels that will be their companions. Especially in the mass and when out of flower, their compact form and dark rich colouring are extremely helpful in securing a feeling of repose in the composition of the main blocks of the rocky region, while their beautiful bloom makes them, when in flower, some of the loveliest of dwarf shrubs.

Here again it must be noticed that care must be taken to suit each kind with its geological require-ment. The genus Rhododendron is represented by three species in the Alps; in those of Switzerland

by *R. ferrugineum* and *R. hirsutum,* and in those of
the Tyrol by *R. Chamæcistus.* Still further east, in
the Eastern Carpathians, is found *R. myrtifolium.* It
is with the two Swiss kinds that our rock-gardens are
mostly concerned, though *R. myrtifolium* is also of
value, and will grow in many soils, though it prefers
sandy peat. Of these Swiss kinds *R. ferrugineum* is a
plant of the granite, while *hirsutum* belongs to the
limestone, as does also the *R. Chamæcistus* of the Tyrol.

Subjoined are lists of plants proper to the two
main geological divisions. It will be seen that in
each genus the species seem to be nearly equally
divided, so that in a garden devoted to one or other
there would be no exclusion of any of the more
important kinds of plants. Those that will do well
in either soil are not included in the list. If in the
case of some plants proper to the one formation we
find in England that they *can* be grown in the other,
it will not affect the general utility of these lists, which
are meant to point out the conditions under which
only they are *found* in nature, and under which they
thrive best in gardens. It must also be understood
that the lists do not aim at being complete. They
comprise only the most characteristic examples of the
species special in nature to the limestone and the
granite, and that have been tried and proved either
in the Jardin d'Acclimatation at Geneva, the newer
garden " Floraire," or at one of the two experimental
stations in the mountains that are on the limestone
and on the granite respectively.

It must also be understood that a good number of

SILENE ALPESTRIS : ONE OF THE BEST DWARF ALPINE PLANTS.

(Half the natural size.)

the Alpine plants that we are familiar with, that are
tolerant of a variety of soils, and that are so well
represented in the best trade lists, do not appear
here ; so that if it is not convenient to supply any
plants with either granite or limestone, those named
in the following lists may either be avoided, or we
may be content with what success we may have in
such a soil as we are able to give them.

There are certain plants of the higher Alpine regions
that are usually failures in English rock-gardens, of
which *Eritrichium nanum* may be taken as a type.
Others in the same list of what we know as difficult
plants are : *Androsace glacialis, Charpentieri, helvetica,
pubescens, wulfeniana,* and *imbricata; Achillea nana,
Thlaspi rotundifolium, Artemisia spicata ; Campanula
cenisia, Allionii, excisa, petræa ; Saxifraga Seguieri
planifolia,* and *stenopetala.*

In order to succeed with these plants they must
have the poorest possible soil; only a coarse gravel
of small stones with a little sandy peat ; such a soil
as will always be poor, light, and porous ; in one containing more nutriment they simply die of indigestion.
The drainage must be perfect. They delight in full
exposure and sun heat, and will succeed either in a
wall or the flatter rock-garden, though here they are
much benefited by the ground around them being
covered with little stones in order to keep it cool.

The following is a list of plants proper to the calcareous and granitic formations respectively :—

SEMPERVIVUM LAGGERI : TYPE OF THE COBWEB HOUSELEEKS, ON A FLAT SPACE IN THE ROCK-GARDEN.

CALCAREOUS	GRANITIC
Achillea atrata.	Achillea moschata.
Aconitum Anthora.	Aconitum septentrionale.
Adenostylis alpina.	Adenostylis albifrons.
Androsace chamæjasme.	Androsace carnea.
„ arachnoidea.	„ lactea.
„ helvetica.	„ glacialis.
„ pubescens.	„ imbricata.
„ villosa.	„ vitaliana.
Anemone alpina.	Anemone sulphurea.
„ narcissiflora.	„ baldensis.
„ Pulsatilla.	„ montana.
„ Hepatica.	„ vernalis.
Anthyllis montana.	Arnica montana.
Artemisia mutellina.	Artemisia glacialis.
Braya alpina.	Astrantia minor.
Campanula thyrsoidea.	Azalea procumbens.
„ cenisia.	Braya pinnatfida.
Cephalaria alpina.	Campanula spicata.
Cyclamen europæum.	„ excisa.
Daphne alpina.	Daphne petræa.
„ Cneorum.	„ striata.
Dianthus alpinus.	Dianthus glacialis.
Draba tomentosa.	Draba frigida.
Erica carnea.	Ephedra helvetica.
Eryngium alpinum.	Eritrichium nanum.
Erinus alpinus.	Gentiana brachyphylla.
Gentiana alpina.	„ kochiana.
„ angustifolia.	„ frigida.
„ Clusii.	„ Pneumonanthe.
„ ciliata.	„ pyrenaica.
„ asclepiadea.	Geranium argenteum.
Geranium aconitifolium.	Gnaphalium supinum.
Globularias.	Linnæa borealis.
Gnaphalium Leontopodium.	Lychnis alpina.
Gypsophila repens.	Meum athamanticum.
Lychnis Flos-jovis.	Oxytropis campestris.
Moehringia muscosa.	Papaver rhæticum.

PATH IN THE ALPINE GARDEN.

CALCAREOUS

Oxytropis montana.
Papaver alpinum.
Primula Auricula.
  „   clusiana.
  „   integrifolia.
  „   minima.
  „   spectabilis.
Ranunculus alpestris.
  „   Seguieri.
Rhododendron hirsutum.
Ribes petræum.
Saussurea discolor.
Saxifraga longifolia.
  „   cæsia.
  „   diapensioides.
  „   burseriana.
  „   tombeanensis.
  „   squarrosa.
  „   media.
  „   aretioides.
Senecio abrotanifolius.
  „   aurantiacus.
Sempervivum dolomiticum.
  „   hirtum.
  „   Neilreichii.
  „   Pittoni.
  „   tectorum.
Silene acaulis.
  „   alpestris.
  „   Elizabethæ.
  „   vallesia.
Valeriana saxatilis.
Viola cenisia.

GRANITIC

Phyteuma hemisphæricum.
  „   pauciflorum.
Primula hirsuta.
  „   glutinosa.
  „   wulfeniana.
  „   Facchinii.
  „   longiflora.
Ranunculus crenatus.
  „   glacialis.
Rhododendron ferrugineum.
Ribes alpinum.
Saussurea alpina.
Saxifraga Cotyledon.
  „   Hirculus.
  „   Seguieri.
  „   moschata.
  „   aspera.
  „   bryoides.
  „   ajugæfolia.
  „   exarata.
  „   retusa.
Senecio uniflorus.
  „   carniolicus.
Sempervivum arachnoideum.
  „   acuminatum.
  „   debile.
  „   Gaudini.
  „   Wulfeni.
Silene exscapa.
  „   rupestris.
  „   pumilio.
  „   quadrifida.
Vaccinium uliginosum.
  „   Oxycoccus.
Valeriana celtica.
  „   Saliunca.
Veronica fruticulosa.
Viola comollia.

FERNS

CALCAREOUS	GRANITIC
Cystopteris alpina.	*Woodsia hyperborea.*
„ *montana.*	„ *ilvensis.*
Aspidium Lonchitis.	*Blechnum Spicant.*
Asplenium Selovi.	*Allosorus crispus.*
„ *fontanum.*	*Asplenium germanicum.*
„ *viride.*	„ *septentrionale.*

THE STONE PATHWAY AMONG STONECROPS AND
SAXIFRAGES.

CHAPTER XV

WATER IN THE ROCK-GARDEN

WHERE water is available, and especially where there is a natural supply and a good fall in the ground level, the delights of the rock-garden may be greatly increased. Nothing is more interesting than to plan and construct a combination of rock and water. Given perfectly bare ground, if only the needful supply of water and change of level are there, with a good store of rough rock to draw upon, there is no end to the combination of form that may be devised; and, having in mind the ways and wants of plants that dwell in alpine and other rocky places, all their needs, excepting only that of altitude, and of the conditions inseparable from altitude, may be imitated and provided. Thus, *Ramondia* can be accommodated in a northward-facing rocky cleft where it receives a little splashing from a tiny waterfall; *Saxifraga aizoides* by the soaking edge of a little rill, and, where this passes into shade, also at the soaking edge, the Golden Saxifrage (*Chrysosplenium*). Then, not far from the rill, but in a short turf of finest mountain grasses, there may be the lovely little Gentians *verna* and *bavarica*, and the taller *G. Pneumonanthe*. So will be devised all the many separate masses or combinations where

239

those two equal claims may be reconciled and satisfied, namely, the designer's intention and the plant's requirement.

It is sometimes advised, in books dealing with the construction of rock-gardens, that where water is used the whole substructure should be put together and bedded in cement. This may be advisable where water is a good deal limited in quantity, but if the necessity for economy of water is not urgent, and if the nature of the rock allows (as it does in the case of the slaty formations and some of the limestones) to have pieces with a flattish surface, that in building up can be set slightly tilted and lapping over one another, the water can be conducted with very little waste, while there will be some to be sucked up at the edges by such plants as those just named.

The tiny rills will have little falls at intervals, and where these occur the water may be widened into a pool; then at the point of overflow the rill goes on again, making its way between the rocks till it falls at last into a larger pool below.

On a still summer day, nothing is more delightful, apart from the admiration of lovely plant and flower form, than to sit quite still and listen to the sounds of the water of the little rills. Their many voices may almost be likened to a form of speech, for in trying to convey in words the sensations received, we can only use those that apply to human vocal expression; for where the water runs between slightly impeding stones the sound is a kind of murmuring; where the path of the stream is wider and more

POOLS AND RILLS IN THE WATER ROCK-GARDEN.

HELIANTHEMUM IN THE MIDDLE ROCKS : MEGASEA (BROAD-LEAVED SAXIFRAGE) AND CERASTIUM ARVENSE IN THE FOREGROUND.

shallow and set with many small pebbles it is a babbling, and where it passes rather quickly in steep descent through narrow, tortuous places the water has a sound of gurgling. And in all these there is a kind of musical note extending over a wide range, from a high-pitched bell-like tinkle to a deep, muffled sonority. It is only when it falls free, with the lesser splash or the heavier plunge, according to the volume that is delivered into the pool, that it loses the vocal quality and acquires a quite different, though always delightful sound.

When the way of the flow and the distribution of the water have been determined and the rocks placed, the general rule for the planting will be the same as in all good gardening, that of having distinct masses of one thing at a time—not a fussy jumble of quite different single plants. And in the case of such a rock-garden, perhaps the finest in England, as the one illustrated, the rule needs a more than usually strict observance. For already there is the interest of the varied masses of rock and movement of water, and to add to this a too great diversity of plant life would cause unrestful perplexity and even some distress. So, in the picture of the little tumbling rill, feeding pool after pool, we have a near preponderance of some of the hybrid rock Pinks, and higher up, in rocky chinks and fissures are nestled the rock-loving Campanulas *C. muralis* and *C. garganica*. Higher still, on the upper rocks is Helianthemum and again little Pinks and quiet groups of dwarf Pines— these few kinds of plants being the chief occupants of

"*Where water is available, and especially where there is a natural supply and a good fall in the ground level, the delights of the rock-garden may be greatly increased. Nothing is more interesting than to plan and construct a combination of rock and water... On a still summer day, nothing is more delightful, apart from the admiration of lovely plant and flower form, than to sit quite still and listen to the sounds of the water...where it runs between slightly impeding stones the sound is a kind of murmuring; where the path of the stream is wider and more shallow and set with many small pebbles it is a babbling, and where it passes rather quickly in steep descent through narrow, tortuous places the water has a sound of gurgling... It is only when it falls free...that it loses the vocal quality and acquires a quite different, though always delightful sound.*"

quite a large space. The second picture shows even broader treatment; the whole middle space between the two rocky paths being a mass of Helianthemum, while in clear distinction from its way of growth is a patch of the large-leaved form of *Megasea cordifolia.* The spaces between the stones of the near path are carpeted with Aubrietia. Other plants are in sight, but from the point of view are subordinated to these dominating masses. The third picture again shows sheets of Dianthus spreading over the flatter rock tops, and again Campanulas in the fissures, while the pool has the Cape Hawthorn (*Aponogeton*) with some of the smaller Nymphæas, and, in striking contrast of habit and appearance, a tuft of the Zebra Rush.

In the fourth picture the pool is larger and the water deeper; it is planted with some of the larger Water-Lilies. In the rock chinks the white bloom of the green-tufted mossy Saxifrages and the blue of the large-flowered Cranesbills are the plants of chief importance. A number of plants that will be useful in the water rock-garden are described in Chapter X.

POOL AND STEPS IN THE WATER ROCK-GARDEN.

THE LOWER ROCK POOL.

SCOTCH FIR ON A LAKE SHORE.

CHAPTER XVI

LAKES AND LARGE PONDS

EXCEPT in the case of Water-Lilies I have often noticed that the smaller the pool or pond in which ornamental water-plants are grown the better one is able to enjoy them. In the large pond, and still more in the lake whose length is measured by miles, the scale of the water surface is so large, and the visible extent of land and water so wide, that one does not feel the want of the small water-plants nearly so much as one desires a bold treatment of tree and bush, and such fine things as will make handsome groups upon the shore and masses in the middle and further distance. If I had a large space of water, with land more or less bare and featureless sloping to it, I should begin by planting a good extent of the coolest and dampest slope with Spruce Fir, bringing some of the trees right down to the water's edge.

The Spruce would be planted as far apart as they were to stand when full grown, but more thinly to the water's edge, so that here, as they grew, they could be thinned by degrees till they stood in good groups. Birches would also be planted near the water, and would show as graceful silver-stemmed trees standing reflected in the lake and backed by a dense forest of Spruce. Scotch Fir is also beautiful near water, especially in hilly ground, and it might be better to plant Scotch than Spruce if the land was very poor and sandy. But Spruce is essentially a damp-loving Conifer, and nothing gives a more solemn dignity to a water landscape than a large extent of its sombre richness of deep colouring, especially when this is accentuated by the contrast of the silver Birches.

If the soil is strong or of a rich alluvial nature Alders will grow to a large size, forming great rounded masses. But some smaller matters will also be wanted to give interest to the lake shore, so that here will be clumps of the Royal Fern (*Osmunda*), and the graceful Lady Fern, and where the path passes there should be clumps of Water Elder (*Viburnum Opulus*) giving its pretty white bloom in early summer and its heavy-hanging bunches of shining half-transparent berries in the autumn months, when the leaves also turn of a fine crimson colour.

The sunny bank of the lake I should keep rather open and grassy, with only occasional brakes of bushy growth of Thorn and Holly, wild Rose and Honeysuckle, with woodland planting of Oak and Hazel, Thorn, Holly, and Birch beyond.

If the lake or large pond is in flat low-lying country, the large-growing Poplars and Willows named in the next chapter will suit its banks or near neighbourhood.

Where there is a good space of water there will be need of a boat-house, or at any rate of a convenient landing-place. It is seldom that this receives as

A MASONRY EMBANKMENT OF FINE DESIGN.

ARCHITECTURAL TREATMENT OF A POND HEAD.

much consideration as it deserves, both in the way of convenience and in that of appearance. The boat-house is usually built out into the pond and is often an unsightly structure, thrusting itself forward in some obtrusive manner and spoiling the shore line of the lake or river. It is always better that it should be a kind of little dock, notching into the bank, or still better, carried further in, leaving a clear waterway of a few yards — the longer the better—between it and the water. In the case of a large pond, or a river passing through a park or any quiet home grounds, the quality that it is desirable to preserve or promote is peacefulness and avoidance of disturbance. Any plainly visible building must tend to destroy this, therefore in most cases it is better that the boat-house should be kept out of sight and should be roofed with thatch, whether of straw, reed, heather, or chip. The earth that would be thrown out would form a bank on the land sides, the extra elevation serving to provide a higher level for some of the planting. This should be a continuation of any natural growth that is near ; in any case some of our native bushes such as Holly or Thorns, and, if the bank is already wooded, a repetition of what is nearest. Where the bank is steep, so that there is a considerable difference between the ground and the water levels, an excellent combination may be made of boat-house below and tea-house above.

It is only in the greater places, where the house approaches the quality of a palace and stands near enough to the water to invite distinct connexion in the form of massive masonry embankment and noble flights of steps, that quite another class of treatment becomes essential. In such a case the boat-house will be a water pavilion, designed in intimate relation to the house itself and the near garden.

It often happens, when a step or any kind of paving meets gravel, that a defect appears that needs careful treatment. It arises from a certain want of observation and care in the adjustment of the points where stone and gravel meet. It is best to keep the gravel a very little—a bare inch—below the stone, and just there, to have the gravel in one level line across the path, not, as usual, bowed up in the middle. It would, for practical reasons, be best if the stone and gravel could be brought together to one level, so obviating the possible danger of a dainty shoe-tip tripping against the back edge of the step; but, where they are level, unless the gravel is of an exceptionally hard and firm-binding nature, heavy rain will make some of the finer part of the gravel run over the stone. In any case there should be no indecision—it is just this weakness of indecision that so often occurs.

The pond-head, so often left as a mere featureless embankment, offers a fine opportunity either for grand architectural treatment or for planted dry-walling. In the latter case, if it has a northern or eastern aspect, nothing could be more favourable for a growth of hardy Ferns. Such a pond-head, with a few buttresses of partly mortared rough masonry, would make a Fern-garden of quite unusual interest.

CHAPTER XVII

SMALL PONDS AND POOLS

It is probably in the smaller ponds and pools, or in river banks and back-waters, that most pleasure in true water-gardening may be had.

Every one who has known the Thames from the intimate point of view of the leisured nature-lover in boat or canoe, must have been struck by the eminent beauty of the native water-side plants; indeed our water-gardens would be much impoverished if we were debarred from using some of these. Many of them are among the most pictorial of plants. There is nothing of the same kind of form or carriage among exotics that can take the place of the Great Water-Dock (*Rumex Hydrolapathum*), with its six feet of height and its large long leaves that assume a gorgeous autumn colouring. Then for importance as well as refinement nothing can be better than the Great Water Plantain, with leaves not unlike those of the *Funkia* but rather longer in shape. Then there is the Great Reed (*Phragmites*) and the Reedmace that we call Bulrush (*Typha*), and the true Bulrush (*Scirpus*) that gives the rushes for rush-bottomed chairs—all handsome things in the water close to the bank.

Flowering Rush (*Butomus*) makes one think that here is some tropical beauty escaped from a hot-house, so striking is its umbel of rosy bloom carried on the tall, round, dark-green stem. It has the appearance of a plant more fitted to accompany the Papyrus and blue Water-Lily of ancient Egypt than to be found at home in an English river. This charming plant would look well near *Equisetum Telmateia*, which would grow close down to the water's edge.

The yellow Iris of our river banks is also an indispensable plant for the water-garden, and will do equally well just in the water or just out of it. Not unlike its foliage is that of the Sweet Sedge (*Acorus Calamus*), fairly frequent by the river bank. I have driven my boat's nose into a clump of it when about to land on the river bank, only becoming aware of its presence by the sweet scent of the bruised leaves.

The branched Bur-reed (*Sparganium ramosum*) has somewhat the same use as the Sweet Sedge in the water-garden, making handsome growths of pale-green luscious-looking foliage, and spikes of bloom that are conspicuous for the class of plant; it is related to the Chair-Rush (*Scirpus*). It grows in very shallow water and in watery mud. The Cyperus Sedge (*Carex pseudo-Cyperus*) is also handsome for much the same use.

Of the floating river flowers the earliest to bloom is the large Water Buttercup (*Ranunculus floribundus*); its large quantity of white bloom is very striking. Where this capital plant has been established there might be a good planting of Marsh Marigold near it

RIVER-EDGE. IN THE FOREGROUND IS RANUNCULUS FLORIBUNDUS (OF BABINGTON)
THE LARGER FORM OF R. AQUATILIS, COMMON IN WATERS ABOUT LONDON.
BEYOND IS A BANK OF SCIRPUS LACUSTRIS, THE TRUE BULRUSH
THAT IS USED FOR BOTTOMING CHAIRS.

ROYAL FERN (OSMUNDA) BY THE WATER-SIDE.

on the actual pond edge. The two look very well
together, and all the better with a good stretch of the
dark Chair-Rush behind them. One point of botanical interest in the Water Buttercup is its two distinct
sets of leaves; those under water divided into many
hair-like segments, while those that float are flatter
and wider. It has been noticed that when the plant
grows in swiftly running water, which would tend to
submerge the upper leaves, they disappear, and the
finely divided ones only remain.

The charming *Villarsia nymphæoides*, with fringed
yellow bloom, though not a common plant, may be
found here and there on the Thames, sometimes in
large quantities. It grows in water three to four feet
deep or even more ; its small, thick, rounded leaves
looking like those of a tiny Water-Lily. Each neat
little plant is anchored by a strong round flexible
stem to the root in the mud. It is well worthy of a
place in the water-garden. I used to get the plants
up by dragging the bottom with a long-handled rake,
and transferred them to the pond of more than one
friend. If a place is chosen a little shallower than
their original home and a stone tied to each root,
they will soon establish themselves and make a good
patch the next year. It likes still but not stagnant
water.

The Arrow-Head (*Sagittaria*) is another handsome
native thing that likes a place near the pond or river
edge. There are other and still better species, one
American and one Chinese, and a good double-
flowered variety.

Frog-bit is another pretty floating plant, with heart-shaped leaves and habit of growth not unlike *Villarsia*.

The Water Soldier (*Stratiotes*) is a curious thing and handsome in its way. The whole plant is not unlike the bunch of spiny-edged foliage in the top of a Pine Apple, but of a dark bottle-green colour and a foot long. It grows at the bottom, rising only to flower and then sinking again. It is more a curiosity than a useful water-garden ornament, but it certainly gives interest to a watery region to know that this strange thing is there, and that with luck one may be on the spot to see it flower.

The Butter-bur (*Petasites*), with its large leaves a foot or more across, makes a great effect as a foliage plant on the pond edge, or where a space of very shallow slope comes down to the water.

The Buckbean (*Menyanthes*) is one of the prettiest of English flowers. Its home is the muddy edge of river or pond or very wet bog; it does not need running water. The leaves are rather like three leaves of Broad Bean, joined into a large trefoil; they stand up out of the water. The flowers, which also stand well up, are a spike of pretty pink bloom; the whole blossom is ornamented by a fringing of white hairs. It is a plant of the Gentian tribe, as is also the *Villarsia*.

The Summer Snowflake (*Leucojum æstivum*) is beautiful beside the pond or pool; in strong alluvial soil growing to a surprising size. It is one of the best of plants for growing in quantity in tufts like Daffodils; indeed in meadow land by stream or pond the two plants would meet and amalgamate happily, the

THE WATER HAWTHORN, APONOGETON DISTACHYON.

GUNNERA MANICATA, IN THE GARDEN AT WISLEY.

damper places of the Daffodils agreeing with the drier of the Snowflake. Here again the addition of groups of Marsh Marigold would come very well.

There are still three important wild river-side plants that are worthy ornaments of the water edge. The Yellow Loosestrife (*Lysimachia*) and the purple Loose-strife (*Lythrum*); both are excellent things to use in large masses at the edge of pond or pool. Of the Lythrum there is an improved kind with still brighter flowers than the type. Here is also the Tansy, a plant that makes a considerable show with its large level-topped corymbs of hard yellow flower. It is a plant that will grow anywhere, but is especially luxuriant near water.

The Water-Violet (*Hottonia palustris*), in the foreground of the picture on page 270, is another pretty native that must have a place in the water-garden. It should be somewhere near the path in rather shallow still water, so that the tufts of submerged leaves can be seen as well as the flower-spikes.

So far no plant has been named that is not wild in England, and yet here already is a goodly company ; indeed the foreign plants for the water-garden are not so very many in number though they are extremely important.

The two great Gunneras, herbaceous plants with enormous radical leaves, something like the leaves of *Heracleum* six times magnified, are noble plants for the water's edge. The illustration shows *Gunnera manicata* at the R.H.S. garden at Wisley, well placed on the further side of a small pond. No plant can be more important in the water-garden ; but its scale is so large and its whole appearance so surprising that it is well to let it have a good space to itself. The Gunneras are natives of the cooler mountain regions of the north of South America, but have proved hardy in England in all but the most trying climates. They are splendid in Cornwall and the south-west of Ireland.

A most important water-side plant is from Japan, the beautiful *Iris lævigata*. It rejoices in rich moist soil close to the edge of the water.

Another water-loving Iris of the easiest culture, liking a damp place by the water, is *I. sibirica*, with its larger variety *orientalis*. If the two are planted together and young ones are grown from seed, which is borne freely and easily germinates, a whole range of beautiful forms will ensue. There are already several colourings of *I. sibirica*, the white being of special beauty, but all are good flowers, with their thick tuft of leaves gracefully bending over and their daintily veined flowers borne on perfectly upright stems. This Iris has the hollow reed-like stem that proclaims it a water-loving plant.

The Cape has sent us a delightful water-plant in *Aponogeton distachyon*, very easily grown in a shallow pond or tank. It has neat oval floating leaves and curious whitish flowers that fork into two flowery prongs ; they have a white alabaster-like appearance and a scent like Hawthorn.

From North America comes one of the very best water-plants, *Pontederia cordata*, beautiful alike in its

NYMPHÆA ODORATA, WITH BUCKBEAN (MENYANTHES) AND YELLOW LOOSESTRIFE (LYSIMACHIA) AT THE POND MARGIN.

RHODODENDRONS BY THE WATER-SIDE.

bold leaf and blue bloom. It flourishes in rather shallow water and is quite easy to grow. The upright habit of growth of its leafy flower-stem is unusual among aquatic plants.

The Thalictrums should not be forgotten ; they are suited for much the same kind of massing on land at the water edge as the Loosestrifes. *T. glaucum*, the cultivated and improved form of an Austrian plant, being the finest.

The large white Daisy, *Leucanthemum lacustre*, though truly a plant for wet ground and water edge, I always think has a flower-garden look about it that seems to make it less fit for water-gardening, where one wishes to preserve the sentiment of the more typical water-side and truly aquatic vegetation.

It would be well that a good planting of Rhododendrons should, at one of its ends or sides, come against a pond, though these shrubs are too large in size and too overwhelming in their mass of bloom to combine with smaller plants. But in connexion with a pond of Water-Lilies, the dark foliage of Rhododendrons, coming down to one shore and backed by the deep shade of further trees, preferably Spruce for the sake of their deep quiet colouring, would be a noble background for the white and tender tints of the Nymphæas ; and as the Rhododendrons would have done flowering before the main blooming season of the Water-Lilies, the two sources of interest would not clash. This would be much to the advantage of both, while each would be suited with a place both fitting in appearance and suited to its needs.

I venture to entreat those who are about to plant Rhododendrons in watery places not to plant them, as has been done so often, on a small round island. I lived for twenty years in a pretty place of some fifty acres where there were three streams and two good-sized ponds. In one of the ponds were three islands, two of them of fair size and closely wooded with Alders and large Grey Poplars and smaller under-wood, but the third and smallest was the worst form of small round pudding of Rhododendrons, about thirty feet across. When ponds are being artificially made it is tempting to leave islands, and if well arranged and planted they may be beautiful, although, in nearly all cases, except where there is unlimited space, a promontory is more pictorial, and favours in a greater degree the sense of mystery as to the extent of the water and the direction of the unseen shore.

If there is or must be a small island it is far better to plant it with an Alder and a group of Silver Birch. The rounded forms of the Rhododendrons add painfully to the rounded dumpiness of the little island. It is better to group them on the shore and to plant the island with something of upright form that will give beautiful reflection in the water, or to let it be covered with non-woody vegetation.

The common *Rhododendron ponticum*, with one or two of bold growth that have white flowers, such as " Minnie," and some of the tall, free lilac-whites such as *Album grandiflorum* and *Album elegans*, will make the best possible combination. If with these there are some groups of Silver Birch, and the

DRIFTS OF AZALEAS ON THE BANK OF A STREAM.

*POPLARS BY THE STREAM-SIDE, WATER-VIOLET (HOTTONIA)
IN THE FOREGROUND.*

whole shows against a background of Spruce Fir, it will probably be as noble a use of these grand flowers as could be combined in a half wild place.

Here, even more than in a garden, where also it is often seen and always to be regretted, an unconsidered mixture of the various colours of the many Rhododendron hybrids should be carefully avoided; moreover, the foliage in individuals differs so much in character, that in grouping kinds together this should be considered as well as the colour of the bloom. There is perfect safety in the group as advised above, its constituents all having the handsome dark-green long-shaped leaves that is so good an attribute of *R. ponticum* and its nearest relations.

Dark heavy masses of Rhododendrons near water are much improved by good groupings of Silver Birches, an association always to be advised; indeed a shallow valley of rather damp peaty soil leading to water, where the wild Birches are thoroughly at home, is the very place for Rhododendrons. When both come down to the water's edge, and the dark evergreen masses with the graceful silver-backed stems are reflected in the still water, it shows about as good a picture of wild gardening with shrub and tree as may well be, and one that is scarcely less beautiful in winter than it is in summer.

Of other trees and bushes of the water-side, Willows and Poplars are the most important. The White Willow (*Salix alba*) becomes a good-sized tree. There are occasionally places where the Weeping Willow can be planted with good effect, perhaps for preference at the edge of small pools. But much more generally useful are the Willows or Osiers with highly-coloured bark, especially the Cardinal and the Golden Osiers. In winter they quite light up the water-side landscape with their cheerful colouring, which is all the more brilliant if they are cut down every year; the young rods bearing the brighter bark. Nearly as bright in winter is the Red Dog-wood, also willing to grow near water.

The Poplars are the largest of the deciduous trees for the river or pond side or anywhere in damp ground. Grand great trees they are—the White, the Grey, the Black and also the Aspen Poplar; but grandest of all and most pictorial is the tall upright Lombardy Poplar.

Sometimes nearly a straight line of these tall trees will occur near a river, and often have they been so planted with the very best effect; the strangely clear contrasting line of straight tall tree and level water being acutely accentuated when the one is reflected in the other.

As mentioned in the last chapter the Spruce and its varieties are damp-loving things. The handsome American Hemlock Spruce is one of the finest, and a grand tree for the water-side or for any damp ground.

Quinces also love a damp place, and, as true water-side bushes are not many in number they should be more freely planted, for not only do they give a harvest of excellent fruit, but they are beautiful bushes or small trees. Moreover, they are good at all times of the year—in flower, in fruit, and when the leaves are gone, for then the remarkable grace of the little tree can best be seen. For this use the old English Quince, with the smooth roundish fruits, is by far the best, the varieties that bear the larger pear-shaped fruit being not nearly so graceful in habit.

The native Water Elder (*Viburnum Opulus*) is a grand bush or small tree, and should be largely planted by the water-side. Any region where garden meets water will be the best of places for its derivative, the Guelder Rose. Among foreign hardy bushes one above all is precious for the water-side, the Snowdrop Tree (*Halesia tetraptera*) from North America. I have grown it both as bush and tree ; and in every shape, and for all garden uses, have found it one of the very best of deciduous flowering shrubs.

The pond water-garden naturally leads to the bog-garden ; indeed the tendency of the valley pond to silt up at its upper end, where the stream that feeds it lets fall the lighter particles it has held suspended and leaves the heavier ones that it has driven along its bed, points to this region of boggy deposit, narrowing to the true stream, as the proper place to grow many bog-plants.

Here, in the case of many swamp-loving things, will be found ready made, quite as good if not better places than could possibly be prepared for them, while other spaces within the moist influence of the region can easily be adapted for others that we may wish to grow.

Moreover, in the naturally silted bog there will probably be already that handsome groundwork of great tussocks of Sedge or stretches of Reed or Rush that will secure the unity and cohesion of the whole place, while at the same time they will make a distinct and easy separation between any such group of flowering plants as one may wish to see undisturbed by the view of the group that is next to follow.

It will be greatly to the advantage of a portion of this region if there is a copse-like growth of something that will give summer shade ; for many are the lovely plants that are not exactly marsh plants, but that like ground that is always cool and rather moist. In the wettest of this would be a plantation of *Primula denticulata*, a grand plant indeed when grown in long stretches in damp ground at the edge of a hazel copse, when its luscious leaves and round heads of lilac flower are seen quite at their best. Several others of the Asiatic Primroses of later introduction are also happiest in such a place.   Next to it, and only divided by some clumps of Lady Fern, would be the equally wet-loving *P. sikkimensis,* and then a further drift of *P. japonica.*

The two latter kinds come easily from seed; *P. denticulata* increases so fast and divides so well that there is no need to grow it from seed. The type colour of *P. japonica,* a crimson inclining to magenta, is unpleasant to my eye and to that of many others, but seedlings of a much better, though quite as bright a colour, have been obtained, and also a pretty low-toned white, with many intermediate pinkish shades.

BUNCH PRIMROSES IN A STREAM-SIDE GARDEN.

The soft lemon colour of the hanging bells of *P. sik-kimensis* makes it one of the prettiest of woodland plants.

Two beautiful Indian Primroses of a smaller size that also like a damp place, though less shade, are *P. rosea* and *P. involucrata Monroi;* the latter seldom seen in gardens, though it is one of the most charming of hardy Primulas. These two gems, and our native tiny *P. farinosa*, should be close to the path in moist, mossy, peaty ground. Also near the path should be a good planting of the brilliant *Mimulus cupreus*, well known but much neglected ; in appearance it would suit the neighbourhood of the Bog Asphodel, the latter in a rather moister hollow with Sphagnum.

In the same cool and rather damp copse-edge the Alpine Willow-leaved Gentian (*G. asclepiadea*) will be glad of a place, and also the North American *G. Andrewsii* that flowers in October, and in the cool leafy mould of the copse the Canadian Bloodroot (*Sanguinaria*), *Trilliums*, and the fine Californian Erythronium (*E. giganteum*), should be in some quantity ; for though they are also delightful plants to have even in a moderate patch, yet their true use is to be in such generous masses that they form distinct features in the woodland landscape. In this way of bold planting, no one who has seen them disposed in long-shaped rather parallel drifts, having some relation either to the trend of the ground, or the direction of the woodland path, or the disposal of the masses of tree or undergrowth, or some such guiding impulse, will ever be content with a less careful mode of plant-

'The Water-Lily's simple form both of flower and foliage seems to adapt it specially for being grown in basins in the ornamental garden... Throughout the history of the world... some kind of walled space of garden ground, cooled and enlivened with... water, has always been made for human enjoyment and repose.''

ing. This applies equally to Daffodils, whose place will also be here as well as in other woody spaces. It is of less importance with the wood plants whose flowers are less showy, such as Lily of the Valley and *Smilacina*, though even with these some consideration of the form of the ground in relation to the shape of their masses will give much better grouping; the result showing as a piece of skilled work rather than as a bungle. As the ground rises, and, though still in cool woodland, is assured of perfect drainage, these dainty little woodlanders will be happy. Further back there will be Solomon's Seal and here again White Foxglove. Presently there will be the wild Wood Sorrel and the native wood Anemone, and perhaps one of the larger-flowered single kinds of the same.

As the wood walk approaches the garden there will be the beautiful blue *Anemone nemorosa robinsoniana* and *A. apennina*, and near them the best of the three North American Uvularias (*U. grandiflora*) and the handsome white Dentaria of Alpine woods. Here also will be our own Purple Orchis and the Spanish Squills (*Scilla campanulata*) with the white variety of our native Wood Hyacinth or Squill, all closely related.

But woodland matters, though tempting, are not within the scope of the subject of the present volume, and they must, however regretfully, be let pass with but scant notice.

The old castle and its moat offer some pleasant places for gardening both in wall and water. In the

A CASTLE MOAT WITH WILD FLAGS AND WATER-LILIES.

POOL AT THE VILLA D'ESTE.

case of this old Kentish castellated house (p. 279) the
originally enclosed space is extremely restricted.   The
overgrowth of Ivy on the ancient walls, and the moat
half choked with Flags and wild Water-Lilies, tell the
tale of the encroachment of nature.   Such a place
seems almost best as it is ; its own character stands out
so strongly defined that it would be almost a shock
to see the last new plants on its walls or in its waters.
Rather one would be disposed to have only the
oldest of our garden plants, Garden Roses, Rosemary,
Lavender, Peonies, and Irises, and in the water only
native things ; the Flowering Rush (*Butomus*), Arrow-
head, and Buckbean.   Incongruity in a case like this
would seem to be akin to desecration.

In some large places there are bathing pools, but
few have bathing pools that are beautifully planned.
A bath in running water in the early sunlight of
our summer days would be a much appreciated
addition to the delights of many a good garden.
It might be a beautiful thing in itself, with a long
swimming-pool ; the lower end in sunlight ; the
upper giving access to a small building, perhaps of
classical design, standing in a grove of Ilex ; or it
might take such a form as that of this pool at the
Villa d'Este, that wonderful Italian garden of wall
and water.

Plants Rooting under Water but Close to the Bank

Rumex Hydrolapathum.
Phragmites communis.
Scirpus lacustris.
Iris Pseud-acorus.
Alisma Plantago.
Menyanthes trifoliata.

Butomus umbellatus.
Typha latifolia.
Acorus Calamus.
Sparganium ramosum.
Carex pseudo-Cyperus.

Plants for Water One to Four Feet Deep

Ranunculus aquatilis.
Sagittaria sagittifolia.
Hottonia palustris.
Pontederia cordata.

Villarsia nymphæoides.
Stratiotes aloides.
Aponogeton distachyon.
Nymphæa, in great variety.

Plants for Rooting in Land at Damp Water-side

Petasites vulgaris.
Lysimachia vulgaris.
Lythrum Salicaria.
Gunnera scabra.
G. manicata.
Heracleum mantegazzianum.
H. giganteum.
Thalictrum flavum.
Primula japonica.
   ,,   Bulleyana.

Primula Beesiana.
   ,,   helodoxa.
Leucojum æstivum.
Caltha palustris (also rooting in water).
Iris lævigata, syn. I. Kæmpferi.
I. orientalis.
I. sibirica.
Leucanthemum lacustre.
Equisetum Telmateia.

Trees for Damp and Water-side Places

Populus (Poplar), canescens, nigra, tremula, fastigiata.

Salix (Willow) alba, russelliana.
Taxodium distichum.

Shrubs for the Water-side

Cardinal Willow (cut down).
Golden Osier ,, ,,
Cornus sanguinea ,, ,,

Viburnum Opulus (Guelder Rose).
Cydonia vulgaris (Quince).
Halesia tetraptera.

A BALUSTRADED WATER BASTION.

CHAPTER XVIII

WATER MARGINS

HAPPY are those who desire to do some good water-gardening and who have natural river and stream and pond, as yet untouched by the injudicious improver. For a beautiful old bank or water edge is a precious thing and difficult to imitate. If it is lost it is many years before its special features can be regained. But if the pond still possesses its own precious edge, and has its upper end half silted with alluvial mud, its great tussocks of coarse Sedges, its groups of Alders and luscious tufts of Marsh Marigolds, it is as a canvas primed and ready for the artist's brush.

In such a case what will have first to be thought of will be some means of comfortable access. For if a quiet bay in pond or river has near the bank a bed of Water Crowfoot or the rarer *Villarsia*, we want to get close to it on firm ground without fear of slipping into the water or getting bogged among the rushes on the bank. So we make a path by putting down some rough ballast and ramming it partly into the moist ground, and lay flat stepping stones upon it, and level up to them. In the very wettest places, or if the path has to be taken actually into the water, some small

IRIS SIBIRICA BY THE LAKE IN THE ROYAL GARDENS, KEW.

Alder trunks, cut up two feet long and driven as piles into the wet ground, will make a durable and effectual substructure.

It is a matter of simple comfort to provide these easy ways; but it is equally important that such paths should be so done that they have no appearance of garden paths. It is not an easy matter to get a labourer to understand that a path in woodland or on water margin or other wild place must not have hard edges, but that, once the needful width is cleared or dug out or levelled, that the edge should die away imperceptibly into the true character of what is next to it on either side, just as it does in a forest track that has been used for ages, but has never been made or mended.

Any hard edge of walling, cement, or wooden campshotting is fatal to beauty of wild water margin, and makes free planting almost impossible. Such edges may be needed in more formally designed garden ground, but they are not only needless, but actually destructive of beauty in a pond or pool of informal shape. A pond-head sometimes must be rather straight and in some cases may have to be walled, but when the wall is not needful and the pond edge is to be planted for beauty, its natural shore should be treasured and retained, no matter how boggy or unsound it may be in places. It is all the prettier if the path does not exactly follow its edge, but only occasionally reaches it; and it can be made quite dry and sound by some such method as that above described at a far less cost than

ARUMS AT A POND EDGE IN CORNWALL.

ROSE BAY (EPILOBIUM) BY THE WATER-SIDE.

would have to be undertaken for an edge-destroying walling.

It was a good day for our water margins when the Giant Gunneras were introduced; for the immense size and noble form of their foliage enables us to make water-pictures on a scale that before was impossible. They are well seen across some little breadth of water like the narrow pool at that wonderful half-wild garden at Wisley; but one would like to grow them in several other ways, one of them being on the banks of some stream that passes down a narrow valley with a wide and shallow stream-way strewn with great grey boulders.

The Gunneras are so overpoweringly large that they dwarf everything near them; their size seems to demand some association with primeval rock-form and evidence of primeval force. Alone among such rocks, and in a valley or mountain hollow whose sides are clothed with dense darkness of Firs, one can imagine these great plants looking their noblest.

In that same good garden at Wisley, now the garden of the Royal Horticultural Society, the beautiful Japanese *Iris lævigata* or *I. Kæmpferi* grows by the thousand—in the flowering grassy banks by the narrow water opposite the Gunneras, by the edges of other ponds, and in a meadow-like space of several acres. In all these and other such places this good plant is doing well. It is certainly *the* Water Iris above all others.

I have often found that among lovers of flowers of the less careful order, there is a general idea that all

Irises like water, and that Irises, with them, mean
Flag-leaved Irises. These are for the most part mountain plants, while *Iris florentina* grows on wall-tops;
and though they may do fairly well on a well-drained
river bank, they are not the true Irises for water edges.

Among those most commonly in cultivation, the
ones for the water-sides are the native yellow-flowered
Sword-flag (*Iris Pseud-acorus*), *I. ochroleuca*, grand in
cool, moist loam; *I. fulva*, *I. monnieri*, the varieties of
I. sibirica, and the noble Japanese flower so grandly
grown at Wisley.

Plants that are distinct of habit and large of leaf
always look well near water; among these nothing is
finer than the Great Water Dock (*Rumex Hydrolapathum*) with leaves nearly six feet long that often
take a fine red colour in autumn.

The great Cow-Parsnep (*Heracleum*) is one of the
best of water-side ornaments. The kind we have
known and used so long seems likely to be superseded
by the newer and still handsomer *H. mantegazzianum*.
The plants of Cow-Parsnep in the picture are rather
too much smothered among other growths, which
hide the handsome radical leaves. It is seen at its
best in grassy water edge or other cool damp place
where it is backed by dark foliage. It would be
excellent about old water-mill buildings.

Thalictrum flavum is a first-rate water-side plant.
Originally a native, and not unfrequently to be found
on river banks, it has been improved and much increased in size by cultivation, and now throws up its
grand heads of feathery yellow bloom to a height of
seven feet or more.

THE DOUBLE POET'S NARCISSUS IN COOL GROUND NEAR THE WATER.

PURPLE LOOSESTRIFE AT THE WATER EDGE.

THE HANDSOME LEAVED GUNNERA MANICATA.

A GOOD POND THAT MIGHT BE MUCH IMPROVED.

A SMALL POND WHOSE MARGINS ARE CAREFULLY PLANTED.

"It was a good day for our water margins when the Giant Gunneras were introduced; for the immense size and noble form of their foliage enables us to make water-pictures on a scale that before was impossible."

It is always well in planting pond edges to have a good quantity of the flag-like native growths—Bulrushes and Sweet-sedge and the best of the other Sedges. Unless the pond is in immediate connexion with garden ground, masses of handsome flowering plants look all the better when they are detached from one another, as they are usually seen in nature. It maintains the wild-garden character that is suitable in places that are rather distant from the garden. *Equisetum* is also one of the desirable water-side plants for this use ; best in boggy ground in shade. The larger of the plants described in the chapter on small ponds or pools will, of course, also do well by the larger water spaces.

Where the pond adjoins the garden a more free use can be made of garden plants. The pond-edge in the picture has been boldly sown with Poppies and Foxgloves, with capital effect. In such a place the perennial Oriental Poppy would also be excellent, and the larger of the herbaceous Spiræas ; the large white-plumed *S. Aruncus ; S. venusta, S. palmata,* and the double Meadow Sweet, *S. Ulmaria.*

Often one sees some piece of water that just misses being pictorial, and yet might easily be made so. Such a case is that of the sheet of water in the illustration (p. 294). It is in the park ground of a place whose ancient gardens are full of beauty, and whose environment is of grandly wooded hill and dale. The abrupt line of this pond cutting straight across the foot of the rising ground on the right is somewhat harsh and unnatural. A great improvement could easily be effected by a moderate amount of navvy's work, if it were directed to running a sharp-pointed bay into the rising ground on the right, and tipping the earth taken out into the square corner on the near right hand; saving the bed of rushy growth and planting it back on the new edge and into the bay. The exact position of the excavation would be chosen by following any indication towards a hollow form in the ground above, and by considering how its lines would harmonise with the lines already existing. The two sides of the bay would also be eased down after the manner of those hollow places one sometimes sees by pond or lake in rising ground where cattle or wild creatures come down to drink.

PLANTS FOR WATER MARGINS.

Caltha palustris.	*Primula Bulleyana.*
Gunnera manicata.	„ *Beesiana.*
G. scabra.	*Iris Pseud-acorus.*
Heracleum giganteum.	*I. sibirica.*
H. mantegazzianum.	*I. lævigata.*
Equisetum Telmateia.	*I. ochroleuca.*
Polygonum Sieboldi.	*Thalictrum flavum.*
Primula helodoxa.	Bamboos, in variety.
„ *sikkimensis.*	*Polygonum sachalinense.*

CHAPTER XIX

TUBS IN SMALL WATER OR BOG GARDENS

WHERE there is not space enough for any approach to such a bog and water garden as I have attempted to sketch in the last chapter, a good deal may be done with small cemented tanks and channels, or even with petroleum casks sawn in half and sunk in the ground. The tubs can, of course, equally be kept above ground if it is preferred, but as I always like to consider all garden problems from their best-looking point of view, and as the use of the same plants would be advised whether the tubs were sunk or not, I will suppose that they are sunk so that they are not seen, their rims being an inch below ground. They will be so placed with regard to each other that they form such a chain as will be convenient for allowing the water, when it is turned on, to refresh the contents of each tub in succession, if it comes by gravitation. Therefore each tub, whether near its next neighbour or a little way distant from it, must be so placed that there is a continuous fall from the first tub to the last.

If the water is from the mains of a company there should be one whole barrel at a higher elevation, with a tap near the bottom whose outlet is above the level of the highest of the sunk tubs. The water should be let into this supply barrel from a height of a foot or so, and will be all the better if it can come through a rose-like nozzle that will help to aërate the water before it reaches the barrel, in which it should also stand some hours (the longer the better) before it is let into the sunk tubs.   One whole barrelful would probably be enough to partly renew, or at any rate to refresh, the contents of the water and bog tubs.

It would be a convenient arrangement for the sunk tubs to follow the line of path on one of its sides, with space round them for bog-plants ; thus forming the section for water-plants of a small rock-garden, whose drier raised portion would be on the other side of the path.   If the little garden is made in level ground, it will be well to excavate the space of the path and the boggy area by its side to a depth of some eighteen inches, and to throw it up on the other side, and to arrange the pathway to come into the lowered space from either end by some shallow rock steps of the kind shown on p. 42.

The space where the tubs and surrounding bog-plants are to be, should be further excavated to quite half the depth of the tubs ; then these must be nicely let in to their proper depth, and adjusted with the necessary fall (about an inch) from one to the other, though each should stand quite level.   Prepared soil will then be filled in to the level of the rims.   It should be of peat and leaf-mould, with one stiffer corner for the few bog-plants that like loam.   Then the rims of the tubs should be closely covered with flat stones that just overlap, laid in such a way that they do not slavishly follow the circle of the tub edge, but rather serve to mask it. These stones may be anything from two inches to four inches thick. Now the little channel must be made that supplies the water. It will look best if it is of the same stones, some larger and some smaller, laid as a kind of rough little trough on a bed of cement, so that the water is carried without loss. There will have to be also a slight ridge of cement and stones between the main stones that cover the tub edges, so that the water shall be compelled to flow onward, and not be lost over the edge ; this can still be kept so informal that the round rim is not defined. The same kind of channel will connect all the tubs. It will be quite enough in a small space if there are five of the tubs for true aquatics. My choice for these would be the little white-flowered *Nymphæa pygmæa*, and the pretty pale yellow seedling from it called *Helvola*, raised by M. Marliac ; then one tub each for *Pontederia, Aponogeton*, and *Butomus*. Other tubs could be sunk for the marsh plants, but if the service barrelful of water could by some clever way of diversion be given alternately to the tubs themselves and to the ground around them, this ground being sunk just below the path level would keep fairly moist. It would, however, be a more effective place for marsh plants if the whole excavated space had on the sides and bottom a coat of rough cement concrete followed by a finer coat trowelled on or "rendered" as a bricklayer would say.

The insides of the paraffin barrels will be made all the more durable if they are burnt out before using.

This is done by lighting a wisp of straw placed in each. The wood is saturated with mineral oil which soon catches fire. The whole inside is allowed to blaze for three or four minutes, till it has a completely carbonised coating, which forms the best preservative from decay. The fire is put out by turning the tubs upside down.

Any of the marsh plants already mentioned will do in the moist area, but in addition other small plants may be named. The yellow Mountain Saxifrage (*S. aizoides*), the Alpine *Campanula barbata*, the North American *Rhexia virginica*, and the pretty native Bog Asphodel; and on the shady side *Epigæa repens*.

The following groups will also come well : the delicate Fern, *Nephrodium Thelipteris*, with *Nierembergia rivularis* and the Water Forget-me-not; *Galax aphylla*, *Shortia galacifolia*, and *Cornus canadensis;* the double Cuckoo-flower and the neat *Cardamine trifoliata;* the lovely little *Houstonia*, with the dainty creeping foliage of *Sibthorpia;* the brilliant blue *Gentiana bavarica* by itself; the violet-like Butterwort also alone; *Primula rosea* and *P. involucrata Monroi* and the fairy-like *P. farinosa;* then severally, the American *Helonias*, *Gentiana Pneumonanthe*, and in the more backward places where rather larger plants will have space, *Cypripedium spectabile*, *Gentiana asclepiadea*, and, if in shade, the handsome American Fern, *Onoclea sensibilis*. Any bare spaces, when the little garden is first planted, can be filled with Mossy Saxifrages, and the wettest places with Sphagnum moss, whose presence is a comfort to many of the plants of the peat bog.

THE SMALL WATER-LILY, N. HELVOLA.

GLOBE FLOWERS FLOURISHING IN A MOIST SITUATION.

Where tubs of aquatic plants are not sunk in the ground their form seems to suggest some rather symmetrical arrangement, but in this case their disposition would entirely depend on what local circumstances would offer or demand.

The little bog-garden will probably belong to persons of small or moderate means, to whom it is an object to avoid costly labour. Many an owner of such a little place has pronounced mechanical tastes and will do all but the heaviest earth-work himself. He will set the stones and make the cemented channels, and knock up a rather close-paled trellis to hide the supply barrel, or even cover it with an outer skin of rough rock-walling that would make a good show on the bog-garden side. It would be as well not to build the barrel right in, but only to make a veiling wall showing to the bog-garden, so that the barrel could be changed if necessary. The piece of rock-wall would be buttressed back on each side of the barrel and a little rough arch made in front for hand access to the tap. Then somewhere there might be a small dipping tank; such as the one whose corner shows on page 307. This is an actual tank in just such a garden as has been described. It is filled by rain water that runs down a path beyond the mound which rises at its back, and a ten-foot length of iron pipe brings it through. It was an easy job to make a foot or two of stone and cement channel with a small catchpit to stop the sand at the upper end of the pipe. The dark hole under the

Harts-tongue shows where the hidden pipe delivers the water into the tank.

Then in such places it is pleasant to make rough seats of wood or stone. The wooden seat in the picture(p.308)looks rugged, but is better to sit on than it appears to be, and after all the purpose of a seat in such a place is only as an occasional perch. Still, if it is the right height, and the back has the right slope, and the rail across comes at the proper place—in this case it was too high when the photograph was done and was lowered four inches—a fair amount of comfort may be secured. The Ivy took very kindly to this rough seat, wreathing the stumps, and, later, the supports of the back rail. Another seat was built of stone in an adjoining bit of garden, with a low back against a bank. On the top of the bank tufts of Thyme were planted that came bushing out and over the edge of the stone, and made a living cushion that was not only pleasantly restful but delightfully fragrant.

PLANTS FOR BOG-GARDEN

IN TUBS

Nymphæa pygmæa.
Pontederia cordata.
Butomus palustris.

Nymphæa Helvola.
Aponogeton distachyon.

IN BOG OR DAMP GROUND

Saxifraga aizoides.
Rhexia virginica.
Narthecium ossifragum.

Nierembergia rivularis.
Myosotis palustris.
Nephrodium Thelipteris.

ROCK-BANK AND DIPPING TANK IN A SMALL BOG-GARDEN.

ROUGH SEAT IN A DRY CORNER OF A BOG-GARDEN. TRILLIUM, UVULARIA, ANEMONE NEMOROSA, ETC.

Gentiana bavarica.
⎧ *Primula rosea.*
⎪ *P. involucrata.*
⎨ *P. farinosa.*
⎩ *Helonias bullata.*
Primula japonica.
    ,,   *Cockburniana.*
    ,,   *Bulleyana.*
    ,,   *Beesiana.*
    ,,   *pulverulenta.*
Cypripedium spectabile.

⎧ *Galax aphylla.*
⎪ *Shortia galacifolia.*
⎨ *Cornus canadensis.*
⎩ *Epigæa repens.*
⎧ *Cardamine pratensis fl. pl.*
⎨ *C. trifoliata.*
⎩ *Arenaria balearica.*
Pinguicula grandiflora.
⎰ *Gentiana asclepiadea.*
⎱ *Onoclea sensibilis.*
Gentiana Pneumonanthe.

The names in brackets are those of plants that group well together or near each other.

CHAPTER XX

WATER-LILIES

IT would be impossible to over-estimate the value of the cultivated Nymphæas to our water-gardens. These grand plants enable us to compose a whole series of new pictures of plant beauty of the very highest order. Their now great variety of colouring, as well as their diversity of size, allow us to make a wide choice so as to suit all purposes; the largest, hybrids of the great American species, for the larger ponds, those of medium size for pools and tanks, and the smallest for those of us who have to be content with a few tubs or small cemented basins.

But certain plants, and especially those that, like the Water-Lilies, have a very clearly defined character, seem able to give us their highest beauty in just certain circumstances. We have to find out the right kind of environment. Beautiful they are and must be in all ways, but one of the things most needful in good gardening is to study the plants and provide them with the most suitable sites and surroundings. Thus, de·lightful as the Water-Lilies are in the margin of a wide lake, they are still better in a pond of moderate size, or even in one that has more the character of a

BASKETS FOR PLANTING WATER-LILIES.

A POND DRAINED, SHOWING THE SPACING OF THE MOUNDS FOR
PLANTING WATER-LILIES.

WATER-LILIES IN A SHELTERED POND.

large pool. If this has a near surrounding of wooded rising ground, not of trees overhanging the water, but at such a distance as to shut in the scene and to promote stillness of the water surface, the pond will be a happy one for its Lilies. Such a scene as Mr. Robinson's Lily pond in North Sussex is an example that could scarcely be bettered. Here are some of the largest of the good hybrids, white, pale yellow, and pale rose, in liberal groups of one good kind at a time, showing the very best that they can do for us in our own natural waters. Such ponds occur by the thousand in English parks and pleasure grounds, and the lovely Lilies only need planting where they will be free from rank growths of undesirable water-weeds, and where they can grow and increase and reward us year after year with their abundant bloom of surprising beauty.

In this, as in nearly all other gardening, if the best pictures are wanted, the simplest ways must be employed ; for if too many kinds are mixed up or even used too close together, the best effect of the picture is lost. Thus if more than one colour or kind is to be seen at a time, it is best to put together gentle harmonies, as of white and pale yellow, or white and pale rose. Pale and deep rose also, with blush-white, will make a pleasant colour harmony ; white and pale blue will be, we hope, a possible combination in the near future.

A heavy debt of gratitude is owing to M. Latour Marliac of Temple-sur-Lot, France ; for to him is due the credit of having perceived the adaptability of the various hardy species of Water-Lily for purposes of hybridisation, and for the yielding of a large variety of beautiful forms. It is to the labours of this gentleman that we owe the greater number of the beautiful flowers that we can now have in our ponds and tanks.

Other growers have followed M. Marliac's example, and now there are many who are working on the same lines ; so that, though we have already a large number of beautiful hybrid Water-Lilies, there is no doubt that we have by no means come to the end of their development, though it seems difficult to believe that anything handsomer than *Nymphœa marliacea albida* and the beautiful pale yellow *N. m. Chromatella* can possibly be produced. Already in the Laydekeri group there are rose and red and purplish flowers ; also the fine reds developed by Mr. Frœbel of Zurich, while M. Marliac promises some of blue colouring, probably the progeny of the blue *N. stellata* of Upper Egypt and the blue Water-Lily of Zanzibar. The difficulty of obtaining the blue colouring in the hardy plant is that these blues are natives of tropical regions, but there seems good reason to suppose that this will be got over, for there are also blue Nymphæas from the Cape and from Australia which will no doubt also play their part in the production of new garden kinds.

For planting Water-Lilies in ponds a depth of two or three feet is in many cases enough, though some

GOOD WATER-LILY PLANTING.

STEPPING-STONES ACROSS A LILY-POOL.

are quite contented with eighteen inches. But if a vigorous kind is planted too shallow, as it insists on having stalks of normal length, both leaves and flowers become unduly spread. It will probably be found that growth in tanks will prove to be the more certain method of controlling the plants, for in some cases when the roots are in a restricted space and can be given a special soil of good loam the flowers are much more abundant. The rich natural mud of the ponds no doubt varies much in its nature, for whereas in one pond a Lily will flower abundantly, the same plant in another is found to run to a large mass of vigorous foliage, and to give very little bloom. This seems to point to the advantage of the tank.

The roots are generally planted in ponds by sinking an old basket containing the root, planted in good strong loam, a soil that all Water-Lilies delight in. The larger Lilies, such as the Marliacea hybrids, which owe their origin to the strong-growing American kinds, will do in fairly deep water, such as a depth of four feet or even more ; while the smallest, *N. pygmæa* and its pretty yellow variety *Helvola*, of M. Marliac's raising, will do in a few inches. This little gem, with its neat marbled leaves and abundance of bloom, is the best of Water-Lilies for a tub.

The accompanying lists show which species and varieties, as at present known, are most suitable for the various uses :—

WATER-LILIES, SPECIES AND HYBRIDS

SPECIES AND SUB-SPECIES

Nymphæa alba.

*   „   „   *candidissima* (the finest form, requires more room and a greater depth than the type, say five to six feet).

         alba plenissima.

„   „   *rosea,* syn. *N. Caspary,* also *N. sphærocarpa rosea;* pale rosy-pink, the earliest to flower, ceasing also early.

„   *candida,* the Bohemian Water-Lily, growth medium.

„   *flava,* pale yellow, from Southern United States, only suited for warm water or the most sheltered of positions outside; growth weedy.

„   *gladstoniana,* a remarkably fine white, colour pure, petals broad, one of the very best.

„   *odorata,* the American white Water-Lily, growth medium.

„   *odorata rubra,* the Cape Cod variety of the preceding.

„   *pygmæa,* the Asiatic white Water-Lily, not so profuse of flower as some.

„   *tuberosa,* another American white Water-Lily, of strong but not robust growth.

„   *tuberosa maxima,* a stronger growing form.

Nymphæa tuberosa Richardsoni, reputedly the finest variety, with very double flowers.

" *tuberosa rosea ;* in the way of *N. alba rosea.*

HYBRIDS

Nymphæa Marliacea hybrids are probably derived from *N. alba candidissima* and *N. odorata rubra*, or from a tender coloured species, or possibly *N. alba rosea.* Scarcely a trace of *N. odorata* is apparent in any of these hybrids, this latter having characteristics quite its own. These hybrids are :—

* " *Marliacea carnea*, very pale tinge of pink at base of petals.

* " *Marliacea candida*, a grand white, the largest of all, frequently measuring nine or ten inches in diameter.

* " *Marliacea rosea*, much better than *carnea ;* the pink more decided and the flowers of finer form.

" *Marliacea flammea*, a highly coloured and very fine hybrid.

* " *Marliacea rubro-punctata*, of the largest size, colour reddish carmine.

* " *Marliacea Chromatella*, the only yellow of this section, a continuous flowering variety.

* " *Marliacea colossea*, reputedly the giant of the race.

The foregoing are all of vigorous and dense growth, being seen to the best advantage in deep water when well established, say from four to eight feet.

The Laydekeri section of the Marliac Water-Lilies appears to have some affinity with *N. odorata* in the form of their flowers, but the root-stock is quite different; possibly this resemblance was subdued in one of the parents. Of these hybrids *N. Laydekeri rosea* is extremely difficult to propagate; it is not disposed to make offsets, hence it is only increased by seeding. These are well suited to shallow pools of water, and for fountains, tanks, or tubs.

Nymphœa Laydekeri rosea, a pale rose colour, darkening each day with age; three colours are frequently seen upon the same plant; comes into flower quite early.

„ *Laydekeri lilacina*, different, in that it propagates freely; flowers tinged with pale lilac.

„ *Laydekeri purpurata*, a darker form of the foregoing, otherwise similar.

„ *Laydekeri fulgens*, the darkest of this section, and larger in size of flowers and in growth.

„ *Laydekeri rosea prolifera* is reputed to be true to its name.

The *N. odorata* section of the Marliacean hybrids have a greater resemblance to their parent on this

A LILY-POND.

WATER-LILIES WELL SPACED AND EFFECTIVELY PLACED.

side. I am disposed to think these have been raised by crossing *N. odorata* with *N. odorata rubra*, because the first of these, viz., *N. odorata rosacea* and *N. exquisita*, appear to be true to this type. These Water-Lilies are better suited to shallow water, say from eighteen inches to two feet in depth. All are sweetly scented. These *Nymphæas* are all quite recognisable by their peculiar, hard, wiry-looking root-stock, which is long and slender ; the roots also are not so succulent as in the preceding.

Nymphæa odorata exquisita is a charming form ; it is a lovely shade of rosy-pink extending to the extremities of the petals.

   „   *odorata rosacea,* much paler in colour than the preceding, and quite as beautiful in its tints ; a profuse flowering plant.

   „   *odorata suavissima,* another variety, the flowers of which are stated to be larger than the foregoing, but of the same tints, possibly darker on the whole.

   „   *odorata Luciana,* in the way of *N. odorata exquisita,* perhaps lighter in colour of the two.

   „   *odorata sulphurea,* a charming Lily, pale yellow in colour, flowers thrown well out of the water, foliage mottled. This and the following are in Water-Lilies what the Cactus Dahlia is in its family, having long, narrow, and tapering petals.

Nymphæa odorata sulphurea grandiflora, a finer form of the preceding, with more vigour.

  ,,   *odorata caroliniana*, a pale, clear, rosy pink.

  ,,   ,,   ,,   *nivea*, a pure white variety, extremely beautiful.

  ,,   *odorata caroliniana perfecta*, a most delicate tint of pale pink, quite lovely.

Other Marliacean hybrids are as follows. These have individual characteristics each of most variable description, whilst to fix their parentage is a difficult matter.

*Nymphæa lucida, growth vigorous, flowers a soft rose-pink tinged with red, foliage very ornamental and distinct ; a fine variety.

  ,,   *ellisiana*,[1] growth vigorous, flowers of the richest carmine with age, much paler when first expanded ; a choice and desirable Lily.

* ,,   *gloriosa*, the finest of all the Marliacean hybrids ; beyond a doubt a grand variety and most distinct ; colour rich carmine-red ; every well-developed flower has five sepals ; this is not seen in any other, and is most noticeable. It causes the flowers to expand more widely.

  ,,   *ignea*, exceedingly rich in colour, growth moderate.

---

[1] This should properly come under the Laydekeri section, which in its buds it resembles, though in vigour it is a great advance.

Nymphæa sanguinea, darker than the preceding and of smaller growth; a Lily that will become more popular.

„ *Robinsoni,* quite distinct, dark in colour with a slight tinge of yellow; a good grower.

„ *Seignoureti* has the yellow or orange more defined than in the preceding; not free in flowering.

„ *andreana,* a purplish red, with handsome foliage.

„ *Aurora;* in the way of *N. Seignoureti,* not so good on the whole.

„ *pulva;* in the way of *N. Seignoureti,* not so good on the whole.

„ *pygmæa Helvola,* the smallest of any of the many fine hybrids raised by M. Latour-Marliac. It is a perfect gem; colour a pale yellow, flowers stellate in shape, foliage small and beautifully mottled with bronze-red; it flowers freely. Well suited to shallow basins, or tubs, or aquaria; six inches of water over the crowns being ample.

N. Arc-en-ciel and *N. atro-sanguinea* are two of the more recent of M. Latour-Marliac's developments. So also is *N. colossea,* already enumerated. Among other recent Water-Lilies, *N.* Paul Hariot is a variety that deserves a place in every collection. It has very large flowers of a clear yellow colour lightly shaded with copper red. It is a continuous bloomer. *N.* Vesuve has very large flowers of a rich amaranth red, and is a free bloomer. *N.* James Gurney, *N.* William Doogue, and *N.* William Falconer; these American varieties or hybrids appear to have a close affinity to those raised by M. Latour-Marliac. The two first-named are after the *N. Marliacea* group, and the latter after *N. odorata;* this is the darkest I have yet flowered of any of the hybrids. The parentage of these three Lilies I do not recollect to have seen given or even suggested. James Brydon is another finely coloured American variety. *N. Frœbeli* is a beautiful rose-coloured continental Water-Lily.

As a rule the depth of water required for any variety may be gauged by the length of the petiole or leaf-stalk. Those with long petioles will be well adapted for deep water, such, for instance, as the varieties marked *.

A CIRCULAR LILY-TANK.

GARDEN TANK WITH A FLAT KERB.

CHAPTER XXI

TANKS IN GARDEN DESIGN

THE recent remarkable development of the Water-Lily as a garden flower has already had a marked effect on garden design, in that an important modern pleasure ground is scarcely complete without its Lily tank. The Water-Lily's simple form both of flower and foliage seems to adapt it specially for being grown in basins in the ornamental garden. The illustration shows a good example of such a Lily pool. The broad flat kerb of wrought stone is in harmony both with the level lines of the water and the flat expanse of grass. Such an edging is far better than the lumpy raised erections of poor design that so often disfigure our garden pools. Raised parapets are only good when they are very well designed (p. 363).

The proper relation of the water-level to the edge of the tank is a matter that is often overlooked. It should not be far from the level of the lower inside line of the kerb. Nothing, except an empty tank or fountain basin, has a much more unsatisfactory appearance than a deep tank with only a little water in the bottom. They are often built quite needlessly deep. It is most important in the garden landscape that the tanks or basins should always have the water at the proper level. In the case of a service tank that is a necessary reservoir, or one whose use is to dip from, it is another matter, but if a basin of water forms a definite part of a garden scheme the line of the water at the right height is as important as any other line in the design.

The third example, with sides alternately round and square, has also a flat kerb, but has a central fountain tazza. The water, as in the picture, is not at the proper level, but much too low. This is only a temporary failing; the dark mark on the plinth of the tazza showing the usual level (p. 332).

Many people will no doubt put forward an objection to the unprotected edge on account of danger to children. But even a flat-edged tank need not and should not be dangerous. In the first place there is no need for any tank to be more than two feet deep, while its under-water margin need not be more than one foot deep. It is much better that this should be in two distinct steps, the outer and shallower part being two or three or more feet wide according to the size of the pool. This would also help to keep the water-plants in their place, as in a dressed tank it looks better that whatever is grown in it should be kept well away from the edge, and be surrounded by a distinct margin of water.

Nothing is better suited to this kind of tank than Water-Lilies, described at length in another chapter,

POOL IN A GARDEN COURT.

A FLAT-KERBED TANK IN A SUNK GARDEN.

POOL IN A BRICK-WALLED GARDEN COURT.

A CANAL-SHAPED POND OF DUTCH DESIGN.

A CANAL-SHAPED POND WITH WATER PAVILION.

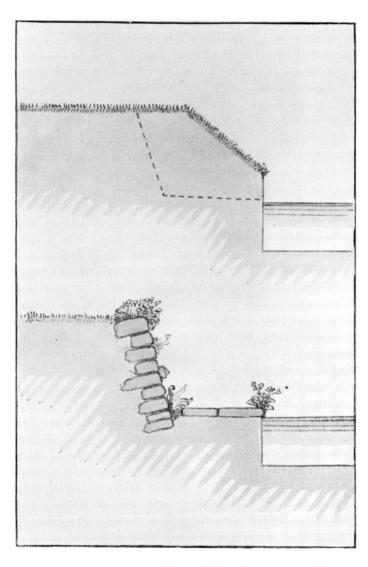

DIAGRAM SHOWING ALTERATION FOR A POOL WITH DANGEROUS EDGE.

and Arums (*Calla Æthiopica*) ; and in tanks of smaller size *Aponogeton* and *Pontederia*. It is quite likely that *Nelumbium* might be grown as a tank plant in the milder parts of England, but it would not be suitable for dressed ground, as the water would have to be run off in winter and the roots covered with a thick layer of leaves or other material for protection from frost.

In another chapter a Lily tank is described in a court of beautiful architecture ; but a much more homely enclosure, with plain walls of brick or stone, a large tank and a framing of handsome flower borders, is a delightful thing in the garden. Such a pleasant place is shown in the illustration (p. 333).

Here it must be allowed that the unprotected edge gives some impression of danger, but this is still more apparent when a tank is set low in a garden and has a steep turf slope next to it. In this case not only is the mind perturbed but a golden oppor tunity is wasted. For, by cutting away the slope and a little more, as shown by the dotted line in the upper figure of the diagram, and making a pathway just above the water-level, paved with stone or brick, and putting in a dry wall and two sets of steps for easy access, a little wall-garden may be had on the land side, and on the water side a choice place for moisture-loving plants such as Mimulus and Caltha, Water Forget-me-not, and those Ferns that delight in a place where their roots can suck their fill of water.

This part of the garden design alone, of tanks in

enclosed spaces, is worthy of much further development. It would combine equally well with upright mortared walls of brick or stone, or with gently sloping dry walls. How easily such a wall and water garden could be made just below a pond-head, with a fall of water dashing into a little rocky basin, then passing under a bridge of one flat stone into a long-shaped pool, with its narrow water-walk below and its wider wall-walk on the higher level. What a paradise for Ferns and Wall Pennywort and Mossy Saxifrages would be the cool and rather damp rock-walling under the head, this being on the western or southern side, and what a pretty and interesting place altogether !

Throughout the history of the world, as it is written in the gardens that remain to us of old times, and from these, through all chronicled ages down to our own days, some kind of walled space of garden ground, cooled and enlivened with running and falling water, has always been made for human enjoyment and repose. It may be said to have been, especially in warmer climates than our own, one of the necessities of refined civilisation. The old gardens of Spain, in the ancient Moorish palaces of Granada and Seville, are as complete to-day with their many fountain jets and channels of running water as when they were first built ; and though, as we see them now, the original design of the planting, except perhaps in the lines of giant Cypresses, is no doubt lost, yet they still illustrate in their several ways that

A QUIET POOL AMONG LARGE TREE-MASSES.

A POOL BACKED BY NOBLE TREE-GROWTH.

simple human need for the solace of a quiet garden, plentifully watered and well furnished with beautiful flowers and foliage and noble tree-form, as shown in the garden courts in the hearts of these fortress-palaces of many centuries ago.

How beautiful some of these walled and fountained courts are, not only in Spain, but in many a southern and Oriental land, and all the more beautiful when they are simply planted with just the few things that seem to have been there from all time. Perhaps a Pomegranate with its scarlet bloom and ruddy sun-browned fruit, and a large-flowered Jasmine; a Lemon-tree, yielding shade and perfume; and, shooting up straight and tall, the pink willow-like wands of the rose-bloomed Oleander; while giving grateful shade within, though growing in some outer garden space, there is a group of Date Palm or a giant Ilex, a Sweet Bay or a Terebinth.

Tanks of water combined with beds of flowers and cool greenery formed an essential part of the Roman and Græco-Roman houses of old, as we know and can see to this day in the well-preserved remains of the houses of Pompeii, where the pillared peristylium enclosed a garden with fountains and tanks. In such houses there was a central main court, the *atrium*— a general meeting-place—which had in the middle a shallow tank with a flat, wide marble kerbing. This was known as the *impluvium* because it received the rain-water through an open space in the roof above it.

The best of the basins with high parapets may be seen in some of the old Italian gardens. Sometimes a fountain basin will rise out of the path or pavement with a dwarf wall of stone or marble some two feet high, panelled and enriched, and surmounted by a coping so nearly flat that it forms a convenient seat, while the water within rises nearly to the cornice moulding. In the case of very large basins they are often and beautifully surrounded by an open balustrade, good to lean upon, while the water remains at or a little below the ground level.

The association of water and trees is always desirable ; in the case of gardens where the trees are of full growth, the tank may be of more than ordinary pictorial value. The level surface fosters the sensation of repose and enhances the impressiveness of the tree masses. Even a feeling of awe may be inspired when the reflection of an unbroken dark mass of foliage creates an illusion of unknown depth. The actual fact of reflection is the source of numberless effects of the highest pictorial beauty—pictures that change from hour to hour, and change again with every altered point of view assumed by the spectator. Any garden ornament or piece of architecture mirrored in water receives an addition to its dignity by the repetition and continuation of upright line. Such an effect is seen in the picture of the eighteenth-century garden temple and obelisk at Chiswick House, where the venerable trees and shrubs, rather overgrown but none the less beautiful, only soften some of the lines of the building, while their spreading masses, partly hiding and partly revealing, stimulate imagination and induce that sense of mystery that is one of the most precious qualities of a garden.

THE GARDEN TEMPLE AT CHISWICK HOUSE.

CHAPTER XXII

PAVED WATER-GARDENS

NOTHING is more significant of the great advance in appreciation of horticultural matters than the careful attention that is being given by architects to garden design. Twenty years ago the architect scarcely gave it a thought; now it closely engages his attention and stimulates his power of invention. And in no part of the garden is this more clearly shown than in the design and ornamentation of the varied accessories—pools, tanks, and fountains—that have for their purpose some delightful use of water. Examples are not wanting in the old gardens of Italy, but, except for certain fountains with their basins, that occur in the design of some of the rather cold translations of Italian garden-planning that accompanied the great houses of classical design built in England within the last two centuries, the pleasant possibilities of water delights in restricted areas, and in close connexion with other architectural expression, have not been worked out until quite recently.

But now even the homeliest garden will have its tank for Water-Lilies, and the capital invention of the paved rill that can easily be stepped over, is gladly adopted and is freely used in varying fashion, always

"Nothing is more significant of the great advance in appreciation of horticultural matters than the careful attention that is being given by architects to garden design. . . . And in no part of the garden is this more clearly shown than in the design and ornamentation of the varied accessories. . . that have for their purpose some delightful use of water." The Orangery seen from the circular water-court at Hestercombe (see pp.355 and 357).

proving a charming addition to the interest of the garden. We are also giving up our dread of tanks as possibly dangerous when they have no raised margin, for we have found out what a good plan it is to build the outer portions quite shallow. In any case no tank need be more than three feet deep, and it is now a common practice to make a wide outer edge only a foot in depth. The diagram shows a useful way of building such a tank edge, with its own little under-water wall for holding the muddy soil in which those aquatics that thrive in shallow water can be planted.

Both sight and sound of water are so pleasant that

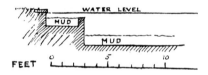

the tank may well be brought into immediate con-nexion with the house ; the paving of the near path or loggia only intervening. Here we may sit in shade and wonder at the beauty of the many-coloured Water-Lilies fully opened to hottest sunshine, and watch the play of light and colour and reflection, ever changing throughout the day ; and see how it all responds to the restraining discipline of good design. And then one looks down the length of the loggia and far away down a long garden path, feeling the extraordinary value and dignity of the prolonged architectural per-spective—and then again back to the pool and its delights.

A PAVED LILY-TANK.

TANK AND LOGGIA: WATER-PLANTAIN IN THE SMALL SQUARE ENCLOSURE.

THE LONG PAVED TANK AND WATER PAVILION.

LILY-TANK AND LOGGIA.

There is a native plant of remarkable beauty, the
Great Water Plantain (*Alisma Plantago*), that has
already been mentioned several times in earlier
chapters. Its name may well be repeated, for it is one
of the most truly ornamental of growing things.
Though it may be found wild by many a stream or
ditch, it is generally so closely crowded by reedy
growths and coarse grasses that its remarkable beauty
may easily be overlooked. There is no better plant
for the most refined water-garden or for association
with the most careful architectural detail. The large,
pale green, plaited leaves, much like those of *Funkia
grandiflora*, whose popular name of Plantain Lily has
also come from this character of furrowed leaf that
both have in common with the Greater Plantain, rise
in shapely sheaves clear above the water. They are
followed by the tall flower-stem which branches and
branches again and bears little white three-petalled
flowers ; the whole mass of stem and lesser stalk and
bloom looking like the most dainty lacework. The
illustrations show how well this fine plant is used by
Mr. Harold Peto, whose thorough knowledge of plants
and keenly discerning perception of their best use is
so valuable a quality in connexion with his matchless
work in garden design. The value of the Water
Plantain is shown in the long canal-shaped pool at
Bridge House, Weybridge, where it is planted in small
square enclosures just within the edges. The same
picture shows the advantage of placing the Water-
Lilies, not in a line along the middle of the tank, but in
patches that are uneven in place and unequal in extent.

The planted rill may be considered the invention of Sir Edwin Lutyens. The one in the garden at Hestercombe shows the most typical form. The wide paved ledges make pleasant walking ways ; at even intervals they turn, after the manner of the gathered ribbon strapwork of ancient needlework, and enclose circular tanklets, giving the opportunity of a distinct punctuation with important plants. Here again, in the rill, with sheets of the Water Forget-me-not, is the Water Plantain. The two little round tanks that show on page 354 are planted with Butomus, not yet in flower. The tall-stemmed bloom is a beautiful thing, but the rush-like foliage is weak. It would have been better if each little tank had been filled with Water Plantain, for not only are the leaves handsome, but the beauty of the whole plant well deserves some degree of isolation.

These long-shaped pools and rills, when in close connexion with house or terrace wall, give the architect an opportunity of carrying out some such ornamental design as is shown in the two examples where a tank, circular in plan and a half circle in elevation, is notched in under the building, the water coming from a spouting mask, which forms the sculptured enrichment of the keystone, and giving the ear the delight of the sound of falling water.

An important matter in the appearance of all garden tanks is that the water should be kept at a high and constant level. Nothing looks much worse or more neglectful in a garden than a half-empty tank. The higher the level—consistent with a practical overflow

LILY-TANK FROM INSIDE THE LOGGIA.

WATER-GARDEN WITH PAVED RILLS.

THE CIRCULAR WATER-COURT.

THE LONG LILY-POOL FROM WITHIN THE PAVILION.

—the better. It should be remembered that with a
high level, reflections are the least broken. In the
circular tank at Hestercombe, in a paved court surrounded by niched walls, the high water level, though
as yet unadorned by any planting, has a beauty of its
own ; it is like a perfect mirror, the reflection revers-
ing, and giving added dignity to, the pair of piers that
stop the wall on either side. This court has a paving
of fine effect ; the broad kerb of flagstone is twice
repeated at wider circumferences ; at the foot of the
wall and midway in the width. Ten rays of the same
flagging, connecting the belts, give two concentric
series of panels that are filled in a regular pattern with
the local stone (p. 355).

The paved sunk garden at Easton with the balustraded pool shows a treatment almost purely Italian,
so much so that one wishes the sturdy English oak
might be a clump of Ilex, and that there could be
groups of the tall Southern Cypress. This sunk garden
(p. 360) is planted, as one would expect, with rare discrimination. It has been accurately felt that the importance and solidity of the stonework demanded a
corresponding strength of character in the planting ;
so that here we find, not soft or herbaceous plants
only, but a good stiffening of shrubby growths
symmetrically placed—showing gardening and architecture working in intimate mutual intelligence—
stimulating, supporting, and adorning each other.

A simple dipping-tank is always a pleasant and useful appurtenance in a garden. One cannot expect to
have the association of ancient Gothic sculpture as in

the picture from an admirable photograph by Mr.
J. W. S. Burmester, but there is often an opportunity
of placing such a tank, sometimes as a distinct point in
the garden design, or it may be merely at some middle
point in the length of a flower border, one side of the
tank forming the paved path edge.

A DIPPING POOL.

A PAVED SUNK GARDEN OF ITALIAN DESIGN.

CHAPTER XXIII

A HILL WATER-GARDEN OF FORMAL DESIGN

WHENEVER I have seen the large formal gardens attached to important houses of the Palladian type that are so numerous throughout England, I have always been struck by their almost invariable lack of interest and want of any real beauty or power of giving happiness. For at the risk of becoming wearisome by a frequent reiteration of my creed in gardening, I venture to repeat that I hold the firm belief that the purpose of a garden is to give happiness and repose of mind, firstly and above all other considerations, and to give it through the representation of the best kind of pictorial beauty of flower and foliage that can be combined or invented. And I think few people will deny that this kind of happiness is much more often enjoyed in the contemplation of the homely border of hardy flowers than in many of these great gardens, where the flowers lose their attractive identity and with it their hold of the human heart, and have to take a lower rank as mere masses of colour filling so many square yards of space. Gardens of this kind are only redeemed when some master-mind, accepting the conditions of the place as they are, decides on treating it in some bold way, either in one grand scheme of colour-harmony, or as an exposition of this principle combined with the display of magnificent foliage-masses, or by some other such means as may raise it above the usual dull dead-level.

And, seeing how many gardens there still are of this type, I scarcely wonder that our great champion of hardy flowers should put himself into an attitude of general condemnation of the system, though I always regret that this should include denunciation of all architectural accessories. For if one has seen some of the old gardens of the Italian Renaissance, and the colossal remains of their forerunners of still greater antiquity, one can hardly fail to be impressed with the unbounded possibilities that they suggest to a mind that is equally in sympathy with beautiful plant-life and with the noble and poetical dignity of the most refined architecture—possibilities that are disregarded in many of these large gardens, with their often steep or mean flights of steps, often badly-designed balustrades, and weary acreages of gravelled paths.

I always suppose that these great wide dull gardens, sprawling over much too large a space, are merely an outgrowth of plan-drawing. The designer sitting over his sheet of paper has it within such easy view on the small scale; and though he lays out the ground in correct proportion with the block-plan of the house, and is therefore right on paper, yet no human eye can ever see it from that point of view; and as for its use in promoting any

POOL IN AN ITALIAN GARDEN SURROUNDED WITH A BALUSTRADE.

"All gardening in which water plays an important part implies a change of level in the ground to be dealt with. When hilly ground demands . . . accompanying flights of steps, the effect is only the finer." Shaded and secluded steps, passing from one level to the next in a garden, are planted with Ferns and Cytisus.

kind of happiness, it can only be classed among others of those comfortless considerations that perplex and worry the mind with the feeling that they are too much, and yet not enough.

For the formal garden of the best type I can picture to myself endless possibilities both of beauty and delight—for though my own limited means have in a way obliged me to practise only the free and less costly ways of gardening, such as give the greatest happiness for the least expenditure, and are therefore the wisest ways for the many to walk in—yet I also have much pleasure in formal gardens of the best kinds. But it must be nothing less than the very best; and it is necessarily extremely costly, because it must entail much building beautifully designed and wrought. It must also have an unbounded supply of water, for so only could one work out all the best possibilities of such a garden.

There seems to me to be a whole mine of wealth waiting to be worked for the benefit of such gardens, for, as far as I am aware, what might now be done has never been even attempted with any degree of careful or serious study. When one thinks of the very few plants known for garden use to the ancients, and to those who built and planted the noble gardens of the Italian Renaissance, and when one compares this limited number with the vast range of beautiful shrubs and plants we now have to choose from, one cannot help seeing how much wider is the scope for keen and critical discrimination. And though some of the plants most anciently in cultivation, such as the Rose,

Violet, Iris, Poppy, Jasmine, and Vine, are still among
the best, yet we are no longer tied to those and a few
others only. The great quantity we have now to
choose from is in itself a danger, for in the best and
most refined kinds of formal gardening one is more
than ever bound to the practice of the most severe
restraint in the choice of kinds, and to accept nothing
that does not, in its own place and way, satisfy the
critical soul with the serene contentment of an absolute conviction.

I therefore propose to give one example of a portion of a formal garden such as I hold to be one of
the most pleasant and desirable kind, and such as will
present somewhat of the aspect, and fill the mind with
somewhat of the sentiment, of those good old gardens
of Italy. And though the initial expense will be
heavy—for in work of this kind the artist's design
must be carried out to the smallest detail, without
skimping or screwing, or those frequent and disastrous necessities of lopping or compromise that so
often mar good work—yet the whole would be so
solid and permanent that the cost of its after-main-
tenance would be small out of all proportion with
that of the usual large garden. These always seem
as if purposely designed to bind upon the shoulders
of their owners the ever-living burden of the most
costly and wasteful kind of effort in the trim keeping
of turf and Box edging and gravelled walks, with the
accompanying and unavoidable vexatious noises of
rumbling roar of mowing machine, clicking of shears,
and clanking grind of iron roller. In the chief por-

SUCCESSIVE FLIGHTS OF RISING STEPS.

THE EVER-ASCENDING GARDEN STAIRWAY.

tions or courts of my formal garden all this fidgetty labour and worry of ugly noise would be unknown, and the only sounds of its own need or making would be the soothing and ever-delightful music of falling and running water.

Thoughts of this kind have come to me all the more vividly within the last year or two when I have seen in the gardens of friends the beautifully - coloured forms of the newer Water-Lilies. Lovely as these are in artificial pools or in natural ponds and quiet back-waters, they would probably be still more beautiful, or rather their beauty could be made still more enjoyable, by their use in a four-square tank in the Water-Lily court of a formal garden, one's mind all the more readily inviting the connexion because of the recollection of the *Nymphæum* of the ancient Roman gardens, of tank or canal form, with stone-paved walks shaded by a pillared portico, and of *Nymphæa*, the botanical name of the Water-Lily. There is a perfectly well-dressed look about those Lilies, with their large leaves of simplest design, that would exactly accord with masonry of the highest refinement, and with the feeling of repose that is suggested by a surface of still water.

All gardening in which water plays an important part implies a change of level in the ground to be dealt with. When hilly ground demands a succession of terraces, with their accompanying flights of steps, the effect is only the finer as may be seen in the illustrations from existing examples. But in the plan under consideration I am taking as an example a place where

ground slopes away from the house, so that it demands
some kind of terraced treatment. First, there would
be the space next to the house; its breadth having
due relation to the height of the building. From this
space a flight of easy steps (the first thing shown at
the top of the plan) would descend to the Water-Lily
court, landing on a wide flagged path that passes all
round the tank. On all four sides there are also steps
leading down from the path into the water. I cannot
say why it is, but have always observed that a beautiful effect is gained by steps leading actually into
water. In this case I would have the two lowest steps
actually *below* the water-line. Although steps are
in the first instance intended for the human foot, yet
we have become so well accustomed to the idea of
them as easy means of access from one level to
another that in many cases they are also desirable as
an aid to the eye, and in such a place as I think of,
the easy lines of shallow steps from the level of the
path to that of the water-surface and below it, would,
I consider, be preferable to any raised edging such
as is more usually seen round built tanks. It would
give the eye the pleasant feeling of being invited to
contemplate the Lilies at its utmost ease, instead of
being cut off from them by a raised barrier. On the
sides of the path away from the tank is a flower
border, backed by the wall that bounds the whole
area of the court. On the three sides, to the right
and left and across the tank as you stand on the main
flight of steps, the wall, midway in each space, falls
back into a half-round niche. The niche across the

tank is filled with Cannas, the taller kinds at the back
for stately stature and nobility of large leafage ; the
smaller ones, of lower habit and larger bloom, being
planted towards the front. Coming down the steps
you see the level lines of water-surface jewelled with
the lovely floating bloom of white and pink and
tender rose colour, the steps into the tank on the
near and far sides still further insisting on the repose of the level line. The eye and mind are thus in
the best state of preparation for enjoying the bold
uprightness of growth of the Cannas. In the flower
borders next the wall I would have Lilies, and plants
mostly of Lily-like character, Crinums and Funkias,
and of the true Lilies a limited number of kinds—the
noble White Lily, *L. Harrisi*, *L. longiflorum*, *L. Browni*,
and white and rosy forms of *L. speciosum*. These
would grow out of the groups of the beautiful pale-
foliaged *Funkia grandiflora* and of the tender green
of the Lady Fern and of Harts-tongue. I would not
let the walls be too much covered with creepers, for
I hold that wherever delicate architecture marries
with gardening, the growing things should never over-
run or smother the masonry ; but in the Lily court I
would have some such light-running creeping things
as can be easily led and trained within bounds, such
as *Clematis Flammula*, blue Passion Flower, and, if
climate allows, *Rhodochiton volubile*, *Cobæa scandens*,
and *Solanum jasminoides*. These would be quite
enough, and perhaps even too many.

The half-round niches to right and left are partly
occupied by small basins, into which water falls,

through a sculptured inlet, from a height of some feet. From these it runs under the flagged pathway into the tank. Two overflows pass underground from this to right and left of the Canna niche, from which the water is led out again into the small tanks at the angles of the paved space below the semi-circular stairway. From these it is again led away into a series of little channels and falls and then makes two rippling rills by the side of the next flights of steps and lengths of pavement. To return to the Water-Lily tank, its border spaces at the angles of the basin would have raised edges, and would be planted with dwarf flowering Cannas, mostly of one kind and colour. The enclosing walls would be about eight feet high, and as groves of beautiful trees would be in their near neighbourhood, I should wish that any foliage that could be seen from within the court should be that of Ilex.

In describing and figuring such a small piece of formal garden, I am endeavouring to show how a good use can be made, in what might be one detail of a large scheme, of beautiful plants whose use was unknown to the old garden builders, for, with the exception of the White Lily, hardly any of the plants just named could have been had.

Had I ever had occasion to design a garden in what I should consider the most reasonable interpretation of the good Italian style, I should have been sparing in the use of such walled courts, keeping them and the main stairways for the important and mid-most part of the design, as shown in the plan, whether the

A WALL FOUNTAIN.

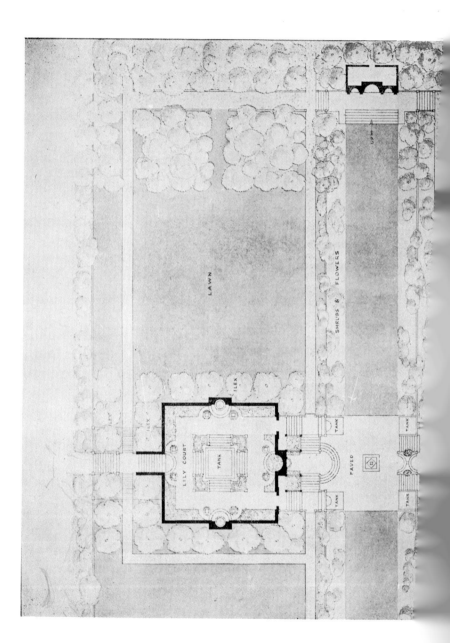

PLAN OF THE GARDEN DESCRIBED.

A GREAT GARDEN STAIRWAY.

formal design was placed on the next level below the house, or, as in the case I am contemplating, at a right angle to it, and coming straight down the face of the hill. In this case, wherever flights of steps occurred, there would be walls well planted above and below, stretching away to right and left, and below them long level spaces of grass. One of these long grassy spaces might well be made into a perfect picture-gallery of the lovely modern developments of Water-Lily, in connection with a Water-Lily court. Straight down the middle of the turfed space might be a narrow rill of water fifteen inches wide, easy to step over, bounded by a flat kerb a foot to eighteen inches wide and level with the grass. At intervals in its length it would lead into separate small square-sided tanks only a few feet wide, but large enough to show the complete beauty of some one kind of Water-Lily at a time, so that the lovely flowers and leaves and surface of still water would be as it were enclosed in a definite frame of stone or marble. Not only should it be remembered that a long vista of successive flights of steps is one of the most impressive and beautiful effects that can be obtained in garden design, but also that important masses of steps are quite curiously in harmony with the most delightful and reposeful of garden scenes, especially in connexion with spaces of quiet turf and over-hanging trees.

Where at the lower or valley edge of these long grassy spaces a descent occurred to the next lower level there would be a dry wall planted with Cistus

and free-growing Roses—never, *never*, sharp sloping
banks of turf. I always try to avoid the spirit of
intolerance in anything, but for these turf banks, so
frequent in gardens, I can only feel a distinct aver-
sion. Did such a turf bank ever give any one the
slightest happiness? Did any one ever think it
beautiful? The upper terrace wall above the level
of the Lily court would no doubt be surmounted by
a wrought-stone balustrade, but as the scheme de-
scended towards the lowest level the architectural
features would diminish, so that they would end in
a flagged walk only, with steps where needful. But
the treatment of this would depend on what was
below. If it was all pleasure ground, or if there
was a river or lake, the architectural refinements
would be continued, though not obtruded; if it was
a kitchen garden it would be approached by perhaps
a simpler walled enclosure for Vines and Figs, the
paved walk passing between two green spaces, in
the centre of each of which would stand a Mulberry
tree. On the upper levelled spaces right and left the
formal feeling would merge into the free, for there
is no reason why the two should not be combined,
and on one level at least the green expanse should
be seen from end to end, the flagged path only
passing across it. And all the way down there would
be the living water, rippling, rushing, and falling.
Open channels in which it flowed with any considerable fall would be built in little steps with falls
to oblige the water to make its rippling music, and
in the same way throughout the whole garden every

IN THE GARDEN OF THE VILLA D'ESTE, TIVOLI : NELUMBIUM IN THE RAISED TANK.

(The Garden as described and shown in the plan is of this type.)

AN ASCENT BY THREE FLIGHTS OF STEPS.

point would be studied, so as to lose sight of no means, however trifling, of catching and guiding any local matter or attribute, quality, or circumstance that could possibly be turned to account for the increase of the beauty and interest and delightfulness of the garden. One small section I have ventured to describe and figure in detail, but only as a suggestion of how much may be done with a limited number of plants only. One wants to see one beautiful picture at a time, not a muddle of means and material that properly sorted and disposed might compose a dozen. I do not say that it is easy ; on the contrary, it wants a good deal of the knowledge that only comes of many forms of study and labour and effort. But the grand plants are now so numerous and so easily accessible that one should consider all ways of using them worthily.

As far as I understand the needs of such a garden as I have sketched, with a nucleus or backbone of pure formality, how grandly one could use all the best plants. How, descending the slope, at every fresh landing some new form of plant beauty would be displayed ; how, coming up from below, the ascent of, say, a hundred feet, instead of being a toil, would be a progress of pleasure by the help of the smooth flagged path and the wide flights of easy steps. Every step in the garden would be nearly two feet broad and never more than five inches high, no matter how steep the incline. If ground falls so rapidly that steps of such a gradient cannot be carried straight up and down, we build out a bold landing and carry the steps in a double flight right and left, and then land again, and come down to the next level with another flight. Then we find what a good wide space is left below for a basin and a splash of water, or some handsome group of plants, or both, and that the whole scheme has gained by the alteration in treatment that the form of the ground made expedient. Then there are frequent seats, so placed as best to give rest to the pilgrim and to display the garden-picture.

Where the lower flights of steps occur we are passing through woodland, with a not very wide space between the edge of the wood and the wide paved way, here unbounded by any edging. Here we have, in widespread groups, plants of rather large stature—Bamboos, and the great Knotweeds of Japan, the large Tritomas and the Giant Reeds and grasses, Arundo, Gynerium and Eulalia, and between them the running water, now no longer confined in built channels, but running free in shallow pebbly rills. Here we have also other large-leaved plants—the immense Gunneras and the native Butter-bur, the North American Rodgersia, and the peltate Saxifrage, all happy on the lower cooler levels and gentle slopes; watered by the rill, and half shaded by the nearer trees. As the path rises it comes clear of the wood, and the garden spreads out right and left in the lower levels of its terraced spaces. One of these, perhaps the lowest, I should be disposed to plant with Bamboos on both sides of a broad green path. As the paved path mounts, the architectural features

*RETAINING WALL WITH PARAPET PARTLY VEILED BY
CLIMBING PLANTS.*

ROSES ON THE BALUSTRADE.

become more pronounced; the steps that were quite plain below have a slight undercutting of the lower part of the front. A little higher, and this becomes a fully moulded feature, with a distinct shadow accentuating the overhanging front edge of the step, and so by an insensible gradation we arrive at the full dress of the Lily court and terrace above.

In so slight a sketch as this one cannot attempt to describe in detail all the beautiful ways of using such good things as Roses and Clematis (among hosts of others) that such a garden suggests. But it is perhaps in gardens of formal structure that some of their many uses may best be seen; for the long straight line of the coping of a parapet may be redeemed from monotony by a leaping wave-mass of a free-growing Rose, with its spray-showers of clustered bloom, and the tender grace of the best of the small white-bloomed Clematises of spring and autumn and of the now many summer-blooming hybrids is never seen to better advantage than when wreathing and decorating, but not hiding or overwhelming, the well-wrought stonework that bounds the terrace and crowns its wall.

CHAPTER XXIV

THE HEATH-GARDEN

ONE of the wilder paths from the rocky places may well lead to the Heath-garden. Already within the rocks are wide plantings of the early blooming *Erica carnea*, and some of the Helianthemums, as forerunners of what is to come in larger masses on the more open ground above. The main intention of the Heath-garden is the conversion of a piece of profitless sandy waste to a region of beauty and delight. The fact of the very poor soil restricting the number of plants that can be used may be regarded as an advantage, because it tends to simplicity and breadth, those precious qualities that so often are lacking in ordinary aspects of horticultural practice.

As in any other special garden whose name indicates the kind of plants grown in it, the occupants of the Heath-garden need not be absolutely restricted to Heaths. The name should stand for a place of Heaths mainly, with other plants and shrubs of the same botanical order (Ericaceæ). This includes some of the most valuable of our small shrubs, such as Pernettya, Ledum, Gaultheria and the several allied species that in gardens are commonly known as Andromeda; also Kalmia, Rhododendron, Azalea, and Arbutus. Near these also, though botanically dis-

A BANK OF HEATHS AT THE WOOD EDGE.

IN THE HEATH-GARDEN.

THE PINK-FLOWERED ERICA AUSTRALIS WITH ERICA MEDITERRANEA ALBA IN FRONT.

A CARPET OF THE IRISH HEATH, DABOECIA POLIFOLIA.

tinct, are the Vacciniums, including some fine North
American bushy forms, also the Cranberries and our
native Whortleberry—all valuable in the Heath-garden.
Two other important families of plants will also find
a place there, namely, the Brooms and the hardier of
the Cistus.

Though at first the poor soil seemed to cause serious
restriction, yet we find, when we consider what are the
available plants, that they are only too many. Of
hardy Heaths we find some fifty varieties in nursery
catalogues ; far too many for use in any one Heath-
garden ; for a good stretch of one kind at a time may
make a delightful picture, while a dozen each of the
fifty kinds will only show as a collection of samples ;
though clever combination, and above all plenty of
space, will allow of the use of a fair number of
varieties. The close masses of the early blooming
Erica carnea on the upper part of the rocky ground
will suitably lead to some breadths of the late-flowering Cornish Heath (*Erica vagans*) of the type colour,
in which an indefinite kind of low-toned pink prevails.
At one point a little stream of the white variety will
come well, and, further back, another such stream or
drift of the redder kind. The diagram shows the kind
of planting advised. The native, and commonest of
all, *E. vulgaris* or *Calluna*, might then follow, treated
in much the same way, with a groundwork of the
type intergrouped with long-shaped wedges or drifts
of a few of the best varieties. These range from an
unusually tall white to a dwarf form looking almost
like a closely tufted moss.

The planting then passes on to the summer-blooming Heaths.   The Bell Heather (*Erica tetralix*) will be kept towards the front on account of its rather low growth.   It would be well to have the type plant in considerable quantity as a general groundwork, with the varieties again interspersed in drifts and thin wedges.   For my own part I should have the type, already variable in its shades of pale pink, with

One side of the Heath garden path.

the white only, and none darker ; when the colour is deepened, in this as in many other Heaths, it tends to a rank quality that is not desirable.   I would also keep the tint light because the foliage has a general greyness, a colouring that in a good mass will be of considerable pictorial value as a break after the greener-leaved kinds, and that will serve to enhance the effect of those of rich green leafage, such as the Daboëcia and others, which are to follow later. Therefore, merging into *tetralix* and carrying on the

ERICA CINEREA, ONE OF THE MOST BEAUTIFUL OF SUMMER FLOWERING HEATHS.

ERICA LUSITANICA, A HEATH OF ELEGANT HABIT WHICH FLOWERS PROFUSELY FROM MARCH TO MAY.

grey and pink colouring, I would have a good patch of
the pretty *E. ciliaris*, a lovely Heath that is strangely
neglected. Its large pink bells mingle charmingly
with those of *tetralix*, and the foliage colour also
assimilates. It should be near the front, for the habit
is weak, almost prostrate, but it has also a pretty way
of growing through stiffer things such as Whortleberry. It is a persistent bloomer, going on till middle
autumn. The Portuguese *E. maweii* is much like it,
but taller and deeper coloured.

The next to follow, and again with a general greyness
of colouring, though greener than *tetralix* and *ciliaris*,
will be the native Ling (*Calluna vulgaris*). It is very
variable, but among a good mass of the type it will be
enough to have the two fine white kinds named *Serlei*
and *Hammondi*, with the double flowered, and a good
streak of the silvery-leaved *argentea*. The Callunas
should begin at the back of *tetralix* and then come
forward to the path. Coming next to green-leaved
Heaths, there is our common crimson *Erica cinerea*.
The colour of the type is not quite pleasing to critical
eyes, but there is a prettier pale variety and some good
whites which are desirable. Grouped with this the
taller *E. australis*, with large pink bells, would come
well. Then to the front will be a large planting of
the splendid white variety of the Irish Heath *Daboëcia*,
otherwise *Menziesia polifolia*. The type colour is a
decided magenta that can easily be spared in the
colour scheme of the Heath-garden, but the white
is a grand plant, and should be used in generous
quantity. Besides its distinguished beauty it has the

merit of long-continued bloom, from middle summer
till latest autumn..

Of the taller kinds there are *Erica stricta*, of distinct,
erect habit, rising to a height of three feet, suitable for
planting at the back of *Daboëcia* and *cinerea; E.
mediterranea* and *E. hybrida*, a dwarfer fine kind
derived from it, early blooming and therefore good
to use with *E. carnea*. There is also the splendid
variety *Veitchii*, a hybrid of *lusitanica* and *arborea;*
with the type *lusitanica*. These, with the exception
of the middle-sized hybrids, are all tall Heaths of a
height of anything from four to six feet. As they are
inclined to more or less legginess of growth, it is better
to plant them fairly close, when some will stand upright and others will incline outwards from the group.

There are a few plants of lowish growth that
commonly accompany the Heaths in wild ground and
that should be also in the Heath-garden. It may be
well to note these before passing on to the bushes
and shrubs that will form the background of the
picture. One of the most useful and, as far as I am
aware, hitherto entirely neglected, is the native Wood-
Sage or Wood Germander (*Teucrium Scorodonia*). It
is one of the few plants that will grow under Scotch
Firs, and, though the name Wood Germander would
suggest that it needs shade, yet it is a rather better
plant on the driest bank in full sunshine. As an
unobtrusive and yet interesting companion to the
Heaths it could hardly be surpassed. Its close tufts
of neat, Sage-like leaves, and spikes of Mignonette-
coloured bloom, take their place charmingly among

"*The main intention of the Heath-garden is the conversion of a piece of. . .waste to a region of beauty and delight. The fact of the very poor soil restricting the number of plants that can be used may be regarded as an advantage, because it tends to simplicity and breadth, those precious qualities that so often are lacking in ordinary aspects of horticultural practice. . .As in any other special garden whose name indicates the kind of plants grown in it, the occupants of the Heath-garden need not be absolutely restricted to Heaths.*"

WHITE CORNISH HEATH AT THE EDGE OF THE SHRUB BORDER.

*ERICA VEITCHII, A BEAUTIFUL AND VIGOROUS
GROWING HEATH.*

the pink and rosy Heaths. A near congener, *Teucrium Chamaedrys*, also a native, but much less common, groups delightfully with the white Irish Heath; the deep green, polished leaves rivalling or even surpassing those of its companion, while the quiet, low-toned rosy-purple bloom, of an excellent quality, shows beautifully beside the large white flower-bells.

With the Callunas, and especially with the white varieties of *E. cinerea*, there should be wide sheets of the common Harebell (*Campanula rotundifolia*); nothing is easier to grow in quantity from seed; and there should also be that charming little plant the Sheep's Scabious (*Jasione montana*) so welcome on heathy uplands. It is an annual, but once in place will reproduce itself from seed.

The paths in the Heath-garden should be either of the natural sandy earth or a short turf of the grasses proper to the poorest soil. These are likely to be *Festuca ovina angustifolia* or *tenuifolia*, *Festuca duriuscula* and *Aira flexuosa*. They are of fine wiry leaf, not bright green like lawn grasses, but of a low-toned colouring that accords well with everything and competes with no other quiet foliage. Whether the path is of these fine grasses or of sand, there should be an abundance of the sweet wild Thyme, while the paler-leaved *Thymus lanuginosus* may well carpet some of the smaller grey-leaved Heaths.

The best kinds of Broom and Gorse, of which the native representatives so often accompany the Heaths, should have their place in the Heath-garden. The indispensable kinds are the Yellow Spanish

A DRIFT OF ERICA DARLEYENSIS IN THE ROCK GARDEN.

Broom (*Spartium junceum*), flowering in July, the white Portugal (*Cytisus albus*), and the Common Broom (*Cytisus scoparius*), blooming in May. These may grow any height from seven to ten feet, and will therefore be kept to the back. Of the Common Broom there are two important varieties, the older Moonlight Broom (*Cytisus scoparius sulfureus*) with pretty flowers of palest yellow or nearly white and *C. s. Andreanus*, in which the lower part of the flower is a rich mahogany crimson. This has a splendid effect grouped with the deepest colouring of the Common Broom, while the Moonlight is beautiful either by itself or with some of the lighter coloured of the type.

Of the smaller Brooms three are important : the cream-coloured *C. præcox*, growing about four feet high, a hybrid of *C. albus* and *C. purgans ; C. Kewensis*, another pale-coloured hybrid of *albus*, but with the dwarf *C. Ardoini*, whose influence keeps the growth low and spreading rather than upright. Other beautiful hybrids have been raised at Kew, *C. Dallimorei* being one of the best. There is also a low-growing variety of *C. albus*, good for use by itself and also for grouping at the foot of the taller type. With those of the Brooms that are of the yellowest colour it will be well to have *Genista hispanica*, the Spanish Gorse, a neat, bushy plant about two feet high. If at the back of the Heath-garden there are spaces that want a temporary filling, nothing could be more suitable than the Tree Lupins. They have a lifetime of two or three years only, but are easily renewed by seed for as long a time as they may be required.

CYTISUS PRAECOX ON A DRY BANK.

CYTISUS ALBUS (WHITE PORTUGAL BROOM).

THE MOONLIGHT BROOM (CYTISUS SCOPARIUS SULPHUREUS) : A VARIETY OF THE COMMON BROOM.

CYTISUS KEWENSIS, THE MOST CHARMING OF THE DWARF BROOMS.

A BOLD DRIFT OF THE RICH YELLOW SPANISH GORSE, GENISTA HISPANICA.

CHAPTER XXV

THE HEATH-GARDEN (*continued*)

IF the place for Heaths can be made quite away
from the home garden it is all the better, though the
illustration (p. 410) shows a good one, part of which is in
view of the house ; but in this case it leads im-
mediately to a wild-looking, shallow valley between
wooded spurs. Where there is no such natural
backing we have to decide what had better be
planted in its place. The treatment of the paths
has also to be considered. If the ground already
has a carpeting of wild Heaths or of Whortleberry
it will be a great advantage, as the whole thing will
then come together much more easily and have an
appearance of cohesion from the beginning ; moreover
both Heath and Whortleberry, if not too old, can
be cut down close to form a delightfully springy
turf for the paths—a turf which will only want
mowing once, or at most twice in the year. Such
a path will also have the advantage of looking
unlike a garden path, for in such a place there must
be no sort of hard or even distinct edge ; the sides
of the path must die away imperceptibly into the
heathy masses ; it must look like a wild path through
moorland naturally worn. Its direction will have to

LOOKING DOWN THE HEATH GARDEN.

be governed by the lie of the ground and by the
points of origin and of destination.   It will further
differ from the garden path because in the garden
design there is always beauty in a long straight
vista, whereas in the Heath-garden the path had
better gently wind, or move as if to take advantage
of the best route through uneven or sloping ground.
This will have to be very carefully considered, for
anything like an over-fussy, wriggling line is an
abomination, even in the wildest ground.

To return to the shrubs that are to back the Heaths.
Among the first in importance will be the hardier of
the Cistus family.   The hardiest of all and the most
generally useful is *Cistus laurifolius*.   It grows into a
large bush seven feet high, of fairly compact form, in
the first five or six years of its life ; after that throwing
its branches about in a pleasant kind of disorder that
mingles well with the tall Mediterranean and Spanish
Heaths.   The flowers are white with a yellow spot at
the base of the petal, very freely produced in warm
summer ; falling before the afternoon, but freely renewed every day during the blooming season.   Of
about the same height but rather less rigid and more
graceful in growth in its earlier years is *Cistus cyprius*,
the kind that is always sold as *C. ladaniferus* in
nurseries.   It has a longer leaf, and the flowers,
though not so freely borne as in *laurifolius*, are much
larger and have a dark red spot at the base of the
petal.   It is rather more tender than *laurifolius*, but
may be trusted anywhere in the latitude of London.
The next most useful kind is *C. florentinus*, not a

CISTUS LORETI : A HYBRID OF C. LADANIFERUS AND C. MONSPELIENSIS.

species, but said to be a hybrid, with *C. monspeliensis*
for one of its parents.   It forms a shapely bush four
feet high and through.   *C. lusitanicus*, a shade less
hardy than *florentinus*, is a beautiful species, growing
two to three feet high ; the flowers white with a red-
purple spot.   These two have green leaves, and would
therefore best accompany the green-leaved Heaths.
C. laurifolius and *C. cyprius* have dark leaves of a low
tone, and a suspicion of glaucous grey which is much
intensified in winter.

Closely allied to the Cistus species are the Helianthemums.   Of these the first in importance is *H.
formosum*, with grey, downy leaves and large yellow
flowers with a chocolate spot.   In a wall or rocky
place it grows into a thick bush two feet high.   It is
so nearly related to Cistus that it is often called *Cistus
formosus*, but it is useful to remember that there is no
true Cistus with yellow flowers.   The conditions of
the Heath-garden so exactly suit this fine plant that a
place must be given to it, though its colouring is such
a distinct break from that of the Heaths that it will be
well to keep it at one end or in some detached bay or
place among rocks where its distinguished beauty can
be enjoyed without other distraction.   But if it is
used in the open it may be further carpeted with
one of the prostrate Helianthemums of which there
are so many in gardens ; choosing one with grey
foliage and yellow bloom.   These Helianthemums are
so numerous and their origin so uncertain that one
cannot venture on botanical names.   In Sweet's
" Cistiniæ," where they are exhaustively described

THE LATE SUMMER FLOWERING CORNISH HEATH, ERICA VAGANS, AT THE WOOD EDGE.

AN EFFECTIVE GROUPING OF ROCK ROSES.

"No race of plants has come to play a more important and valuable part in the furnishing of the modern woodland and water garden than the Asiatic Primulas... On the whole they are an easy race, well mannered, of good temperament, and never troublesome to manage, either in the more ordered and disciplined places or in the more unconventional surroundings of the woodland or water-side where they are probably more at home." The group of waterside plants includes Primula Florindae.

and admirably figured in colour, we find no less than seventy species; quite two-thirds of this number being of garden value. Though it is generally thought that the kinds we find in nurseries come mainly from *Helianthemum vulgare*, the common Rock Rose, yet there is so much variety of foliage that there is probably an admixture of other species, for of both the grey-leaved and the dark-leaved kinds there are some leaves long and almost linear, and others roundish or at least broad in proportion to length. The colour of the flowers ranges from white, through pale pink, to deep pink and rose; and from pale to full yellow, and on to deep orange and pure scarlet. For the Heath-garden the most suitable will be some of the grey-leaved whites and pale pinks to go with the greyer, pink-belled Heaths, besides the grey-leaved yellow already mentioned as a companion to *Helianthemum formosum*.

Other shrubs that will be good companions to the Heaths, and are botanically related to them, are some of those that are commonly known in gardens as Andromedas. Of these the most beautiful is *Zenobia pulverulenta*, also called *Andromeda speciosa*. The flowers are large white waxy bells much like Lily of the Valley, and the foliage is covered with a whitish powdery bloom that gives it a distinctly grey colour and that makes it suitable for placing near the greyest of the Heaths. *Pieris floribunda*, about five feet high, with dark leaves and blooming in April, may well be placed as a backing to some of the early Heaths. *Leucothoë Catesbæi*, and the smaller *L. axillaris* which

LEUCOTHOË CATESBÆI.

much resembles it, will come well with the Heaths of
middle and late summer. Both are happiest in a
rather cool place in slight shade.

The Heaths of darkest green will be most suitably
backed with *Pernettya*, another related shrub ; either
the type *P. mucronata* or some of the free-berrying
varieties. The Alpenrose (*Rhododendron ferruginium*)
is one of the very best of small Heath-garden shrubs,
and further back should be the rather larger *R.
myrtifolium*, growing about five feet high. *R. præcox*
blooms with the earliest Heaths, and may well be
planted with them. It grows to a height of four or
five feet. At any points where taller shrubs would
come well or shelter is desired, Arbutus will be in
place and should be planted in bold groups. There
are still some small shrubs that should have a place,
among them the Ledums. Of these the most useful
are the small *L. thymifolium* with its pretty rosy
flower-buds, and the larger *L. palustre*; the foliage
of the latter has a dusky darkness that sets off the
colouring of any near plants. It should be near the
path, so that a leaf may easily be picked and bruised
and the good, wholesome scent—something between
myrtle and turpentine—be enjoyed.

It will be desirable, where the actual Heaths end,
to come to some special kinds of others of the beautiful shrubs of the same botanical order—namely,
Kalmia, Rhododendron, and Azalea. A little grove
of the sweet Candleberry Gale (*Myrica cerifera*), growing shoulder high and, like the Ledum, sweet—even
sweeter—to pick and bruise, might well come next

as a change of scene and manner of enjoyment. In the middle of such a grove a good group of *Kalmia latifolia* would be well placed.

In such a garden, bearing in mind that the Heaths are to dominate, it would be well to deny oneself the use of brilliant Azaleas of the *sinensis* (*mollis*) and Ghent classes, and the usual hybrid Rhododendrons. The Rhododendrons are so masterful in mass, and the Azaleas in colour, that they need special places of their own that had better be somewhere away from the less bulky and showy occupants of the Heath-garden. It is better that the continuation of this should be of some of the more beautiful of the species and a few of the more refined of the hybrids ; so that, while these are still used in pictorial fashion, one may at the same time have the full enjoyment of each as an individual. Therefore, after the Kalmias I should have some bushes of the Californian Azalea (*A. occidentalis*), a shrub but little known in gardens and yet of quite extraordinary beauty. The flowers, white or faintly rosy, are large and yet of the most refined shape ; the leaves are long and lustrous, and have the truly ornamental quality that is lacking in the Ghent varieties. Its only fault is that it is never very full of bloom.

In this part of the garden should be also the handsome species *Rhododendron Vaseyi* from the northern United States, *R. yunnanense* and *R. rubiginosum*, both from China, and the dwarf *R. caucasicum*. As will be seen in the illustrations, some of these are what we should in gardens class as Azaleas ; but

RHODODENDRON VASEYI.

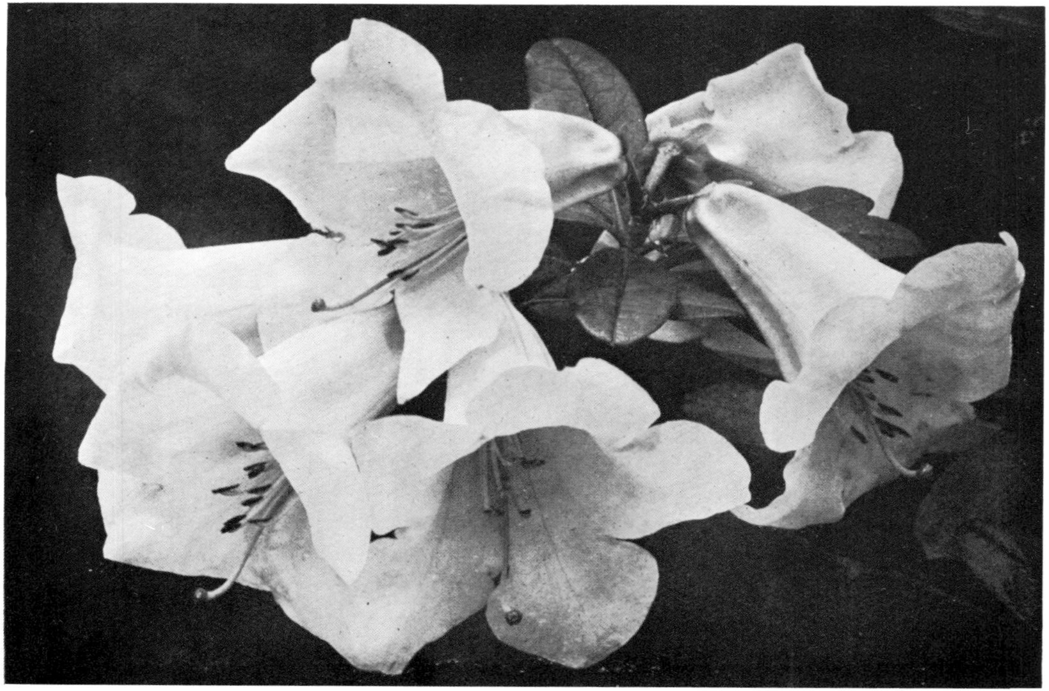

RHODODENDRON VICTORIANUM.

botanists seem to have discarded the name Azalea and put all under Rhododendron. Still, for garden purposes and as popular names the distinction is useful and should be retained.

The species just named being of whitish or tender colouring may be in the same region. They will look well grouped with the bush Vacciniums, *V. pennsylvanium* and *V. corymbosum*, whose leaves turn a splendid colour, almost scarlet, in autumn. Of the larger Rhododendrons the ones most suitable for association with these pretty species will be the hardy hybrids of the tender *R. Aucklandi*. They have the bloom of large size and of the wonderful substance and texture which is visible in the picture showing a cluster of bloom of *R. Victorianum*. This beautiful variety is not hardy enough to trust out of doors, but is shown to indicate the general appearance of some of these fine hybrids. Though so large in size, they are of the utmost refinement.

For large shrubs at the back of the Heath-garden, those that will be found the most useful are the Common Juniper in the greyer region, and Arbutus where the leaf colouring is green.

For Heaths, and all the plants and shrubs advised for the Heath-garden, it is of course an advantage if the soil is naturally peaty or can be made so, though they will also do well on any light soil—even the very sandiest—though in this some leaf-mould will be a help. Only *Erica carnea* is tolerant of lime and does well in any soil.

CHAPTER XXVI

WOODLAND GARDENING

WHEN a garden adjoins woodland many are the opportunities for effective planting. Where the wood is large and trees grow thinly it is a precious opportunity for planting Daffodils in quantity. In a large space they are all the more interesting if they are shown in a natural sequence of kinds, or in some way that shows how the more typical Narcissi and their hybrids merge one into another. The largest and most effective are the Trumpets; planted sometimes thickly in masses and then in straggling groups, according to the nature of the ground, they have the best effect. One kind at a time, and such as the good old Horsfieldi may be the best for the wood, then passing on to the *Incomparabilis* and their hybrids with poeticus, the beautiful Barri and Leedsi varieties, and finally to the pure white poeticus. There is one fine Pyrennean kind, *N. pallidus præcox*, that so much dislikes garden culture that it actually dies out in good cultivation. This is the experience not only in the writer's case, but in that of practical nurserymen. But put it in the wild, and it increases not only by the bulb but by seed, which is freely produced and is carried about by birds, for we find young plants, not only within the original patch but

THE PATH FROM THE GARDEN INTO THE WOODLAND FLANKED BY FERNS AND
COLONIES OF PRIMULAS

AND CARPET OF BUNCH PRIMROSES.

here and there, some of them a hundred yards away. It is a trumpet of moderate size of a rather pale buttery yellow colouring. The place where they are growing so freely is on hilly ground with a thin soil of peaty sand in the extreme south-west of Surrey. Their dying foliage is soon covered by the natural growth of Bracken. Beyond the Daffodils, still in thin woodland, is a wide planting of Lily of the Valley, which spreads willingly in the light soil and is nourished by the yearly natural mulch of dead leaves. Many are the ways in which the approaches to the woodland planting may be made. There is a fine strain of Bunch Primroses in trade that bears planting in masses in the nearer regions, rather than in the more distant wild. It is in colourings of whites and yellows that go happily together. It is later blooming than the true Primroses, for it is not at its best till the middle of May. They are in a place where there were one or two well-grown Oaks ; some Cobnuts were added because it had always been observed in the near-by hilly copses, that the wild Primroses were always finest where these had the overhead shelter of occasional Oaks and a closer planting of Hazel. But these garden Primroses want good cultivation, and though they have been grown in the same place for many years their beds are refreshed every year with a good dressing of well-rotted leaf-mould.

In the face of the wood and running into it here and there are some drifts and bold patches of the pure white Foxglove. The groups are placed so that they always have some background of dusky mystery. In October some self-sown plants from seed of the year before are placed as the foundation of the group, with smaller ones between. When the seed is ripe a little of it is sown within the spaces of the intended groups, and when all the seed is gathered the old plants are pulled up and taken away. Then the hardy Ferns that accompany them appear to take their place, and spread their fronds over what would have been patches of unsightly emptiness. One of the shady walks has a slightly rising bank that has been cleared of its native Bracken and Brambles and shows a refreshing mass of tender greenery. It is *Smilacina bifolia*, a precious plant for light soils. It may be left untouched for many years, forming a perfect carpet of its neat foliage, with the pretty spikes of white bloom in June. No other flowering plant is near, and it is all the better and all the more interesting for its isolation, which is only modified by the presence in the upper part of the bank of a few of that loveliest of our native ferns, the Dilated Shield Fern.

Among the various ways of passing from garden to woodland one of the best is by a planting of Rhododendron. It should be remembered that though the Rhododendron is a mass of coloured bloom in early summer, yet for the rest of the year it is for foliage only. It is therefore a good plan to keep some of the older kinds that are derived from *R. ponticum* in the foreground ; for they have the dark foliage and high polish that is so good in the winter months, in contrast to the leaves of many fine kinds, hybrids of *Catawbiense*, that are not only of a poorer colour but that show distress in very hard weather by the hanging down of their leaves. For the best effect it will be well that the Rhododendrons

A SPRING CARPET OF DAFFODILS.

AZALEAS IN A WOODLAND CLEARING.

shall begin with some of tender colouring, pale and rich pink, following on to good reds. For this they could begin with such as Pink Pearl and Alice, passing on to deep rosy reds, such as the good old Lady Eleanor Cathcart and Mrs. R. S. Holford. These may lead to the pure reds, such as Doncaster and the grand red Baron de Bruin. There are a number of fine things of more ordinary red colourings, but those mentioned are without the magenta taint that is avoided by the more sensitive eye. Then it may be well to have some of the pure whites, and after these, where the shade deepens, some of the fine old kinds of pale purplish colouring shading to nearly white, such as *Album grandiflorum* and *Album elegans*. These in time grow to a considerable height and combine happily with the tree growths of the actual woodland.

Although Rhododendrons and Azaleas are so closely related, yet their colourings and habit of growing are so dissimilar that in the woodland garden they are best kept apart. Another way into the wood should be given to the Azaleas. There are the early blooming *A. mollis* varieties, flowering in May so luxuriantly that the bushes become almost smothered in bloom. But the Ghent Azaleas are the ones best suited to advance into the closer woodland. In fact, though they are thankful for the near shelter, they are best suited by a clearing among the actual tree growth. A good space should be given to the old *A. pontica*, now sometimes forgotten among the many beautiful hybrids, but in a mass it tones well into the woody background, while for sweetness and wealth of bloom it is indispensable, and is so early that it lengthens the Azalea time by nearly a fortnight. The number of beautiful kinds is almost bewildering, but there is a double deep pink Fama which is indispensable, and so prolific that the mass of bloom entirely covers the bush. There are many beautiful pinks, the half - double Rosetta, varieties of Marie Ardente, Bijou de Gendbrugge, and others. Among those of orange colouring are Princeps and the resplendent Gloria Mundi—of strong reds Grandeur Triomphant and Sang de Gendbrugge. But the fine kinds are so many that it is much best to visit a nursery with a reputation for Rhododendrons as well as Azaleas and see them at flowering time, not forgetting to examine the beds of seedlings, where many choice kinds, as yet unnamed, are sure to be found. The Azaleas are planted fairly well apart, for many of them grow into pretty little tree forms that can only be properly seen if they can be visible nearly all round, and none of them care to be crowded. Especially to be avoided is the unhappy bed of Azaleas, too often to be seen in gardens, where a number of kinds are seen painfully jostling one another, without any consideration for colouring or habit. Partly among the Azaleas, and rejoicing in the same kind of woodland clearing, there are the Vacciniums, some of the precious things that have come to us from North America ; *V. corymbosum* and *V. pennsylvanicum*, neat shrubs allied to the native Whortleberry ; also the Candleberry Gale, *Myrica cerifera*, a near relation of our Bog Myrtle. Clusters of little grains of a waxy nature come among the inconspicuous flowers ; these are collected by the people of New England and made into candles looking like greenish wax, which are said to burn with an aromatic scent. Some of the Cistus kinds are also among the Azaleas and enjoy the shelter of the woodland clearing. The hardiest of all is *C. laurifolius* ; in some of the heathlands of West Surrey it has become naturalised by self-sowing, much to the delight and wonder of the roving botanist. The taller growing *C. cyprius*, which is often sold as *C. ladaniferus*, is also among the Azaleas ; its long, arching branches coming well among the flowering bushes. The less hardy *C. florentinus* is also there. We cover it with some cut bushy stuff for the winter as it is rather tender. A lovely Azalea that should not be forgotten is *A. occidentalis*, a native of California. When the Ghent kinds are going over, this beautiful thing is at its best. It is a flower of singular purity and distinction, white or with a flush of tenderest pink ; the leaves, also, are of special beauty, for they have a polished surface such as is unknown among the more familiar kinds.

Some of the Lilies are of wonderful beauty in the woodland. In no other garden use are they seen to such advantage, for they seem to give of their best when they are given a place where there is a surrounding of quiet conditions, and in some cases of isolation. Such a setting seems to be specially sympathetic to the stately *Lilium giganteum*. It is at its best in thin woodland in a naturally rich soil, where in some places it has become naturalised. But even in a light soil, if a place is well prepared, such as a hole, wide and deep, packed with vegetable rubbish such as Dahlia tops and other yearly stuff from the flower borders, it will provide the

rich slowly decaying humus that this grand Lily requires. In this they can be grown to perfection and
may rise to a height of eleven feet. Unlike the greater
number of the Lilies it must not be planted deeply ; the
top of the great bulb should be just above ground, and
at the most it may have a loose winter covering of dead
leaves. It readily forms offsets and also seed in good
quantity, but the small bulbs that are formed at the base
are the better means of increase, and in two years' time
they will be of flowering strength. A group of related
Lilies that are also to be advised for openings in thin
woodland are *L. croceum* and its congeners of the
davuricum and *umbellatum* classes, including what are
known as Herring Lilies by the Dutch. They are all of
deep yellow or orange colouring. The Tiger Lilies, so
easily grown in some places, may well accompany them.
But all are thankful for careful planting in well-prepared
places and for a yearly mulching of decayed leaf-mould
with some suitable enrichment. *Lilium auratum*, and
especially its fine variety *platyphyllum*, is perhaps the
best Lily of all for woodland edges. It is a fine thing
to have among Rhododendrons, forming in September
quite new and distinct points of interest. But it is in
the earlier summer that the shady depths will be fullest
of beauty and interest. A fine lesson and example is a
wood of wild Bluebells in May ; it shows the value of
doing one thing at a time, and doing it largely and
thoroughly well. But though planted wood gardens
cannot give the space for such great shows as we see in
the wild, yet they remind us of the use in shade of their
near relations the Spanish Squills (*Scilla campanulata*),

COLONIES OF FERNS AND BAMBOOS AFFORDING A CHARMING VARIETY OF COLOUR AND
TEXTURE IN THE WOODLAND.

BOLD FOLIAGE PLANTS, SENECIOS AND BOCCONIAS AT THE WOOD EDGE FOR PICTURESQUE EFFECTS.

much like our Bluebells in general appearance, and well
adapted for planting in some quantity in shady places.
They are in three colourings ; the purplish-blue of our
Bluebells, a quiet kind of pink, and a pure white. Of the
last there are some fine forms, with large bells of great
substance and a larger number than usual of flowers on
the spike. Drifts of these good flowers, accompanied
by Solomon's Seal, form a pleasing combination, with
more Solomon's Seal beyond, passing to a wide planting
of our best hardy Ferns. A whole length of a woodland
path should be given to these Ferns. Where it passes
through a damp place the Lady Fern (*Athyrium Filix-
fœmina*) will luxuriate. It is one of the most graceful
of British Ferns, with fronds of a pale green colour and
of a rather fragile appearance. Its only defect is that
it is the earliest to show the destructive effects of the
early autumn frosts. But another damp-loving Fern,
Blechnum spicant, the Northern Hard Fern, is hardy
and persistent. It is a much smaller plant and can be
used in good masses near the path. But the grandest
of the Ferns for a damp place is the Royal Fern *Osmunda
regalis*. It is not a Fern to plant in quantity, for it is so
distinctive, with its large, rather unfern-like fronds, and
its separate flowering spikes, that a few only, planted a
little way apart, can be better seen and more critically
observed. But the loveliest of the larger native Ferns
is without doubt the Dilated Shield Fern *Lastrea
dilatata*. It deserves to have more than one place, and
it should not be crowded. The whole form of the plant
is a delight, the few fronds are carried with perfect grace,
and their detail is of the loveliest. This also should be

placed so that the individual plants scarcely touch each other, with here and there one example quite isolated. The drier part of the wood walk is the place for the Black Maidenhair Spleenwort (*Asplenium Adiantum nigrum*), a rather small plant. It will look well if it is accommodated with some kind of slight stone-work coming barely out of the ground, and will be all the better for such a setting. A larger kind of this Fern is grown in the South of France and imported for florists' use. It is known in the shops as French Fern. The woodland walk is not the place for masses of showy flowers, it is rather for solitary sauntering and the leisurely refreshment of a quiet mind. It is a place for some of the less common native plants, such as the sweet-scented Butterfly Orchis (*Habenaria bifolia*), for the neat little *Pyrola*, for the curious Twayblade (*Listera ovata*), and the four-leaved Herb Paris ; small groups or even single plants of these, with larger patches of Butcher's Broom (*Ruscus aculeatus*) and the handsome Woodrush (*Luzula sylvatica*), and also, but not too close to the path, the wild Garlic (*Allium ursinum*) ; a fine plant, with its brightly polished leaves and white bloom ; but better to look at than to handle on account of its rank garlicky smell. A place for Trilliums must not be forgotten ; they will come best among the groups of Ferns, where their large white flowers show up finely. The North American Bramble *Rubus nutkanus* is an admirable thing for the woodland. It seems to be much neglected, for it is seldom seen in gardens. Its growth is much like that of the Raspberry, with woody canes three to four feet high. The flowers are like large single white Roses, nearly resembling those of *Rubus deliciosus*, and the large, fresh green leaves are like those of the Vines that are wide and undivided. It takes readily to any shady place, where its shallow roots will run freely in a natural thin soil surface of decaying leaves. A good backing of male Fern suits it well. When the woodland path comes out into more open copse there are some small flowering trees that will always give pleasure and will look quite at home among the native growths, especially if these are Birches and Junipers and Bracken, with little Oaks and a background of Scotch Pine. *Amelanchier canadensis* is a little tree with small cherry-like bloom in quantity in early summer. It has the generous quality of distributing its seed, no doubt by the agency of birds, for when it has flowered and fruited, young seedlings will appear, not only close at hand but some distance away. There is a region of hilly ground in south-west Surrey where it was planted in a wood adjoining park land some time near the middle of the last century. It has become naturalised in neighbouring woodlands within a radius of a good two miles from where it was originally planted. The Bird Cherry (*Prunus Padus*) is another of these pretty small trees, and yet another is the Snowdrop Tree *Halesia tetraptera*. This is usually grown as a large bush, with several rods from the root, like a Hazel, but sometimes it will shoot up with a single stem and take a true tree form, with a straight trunk rising straight up to something like forty feet.

To return to the shady woodland path, one of the most precious things for careful planting, where the

ground is cool and the shade is not too deep, but is
such as will give a good background, is the lovely blue
Poppy *Meconopsis betonicifolia Baileyi.* But, like
many other good things, it should not be overdone.
Twenty plants, in their groups of four or five, with single
ones between, will make a better show than a hundred
huddled together. It is impossible to describe such
planting precisely, but this work in woody places seems
to demand the artist's eye for balance and proportion.
This wonderful Poppy varies in colour from a nearly
pure blue, in shades both light and dark, to lilac or
purplish tints. It is best to sacrifice these, pulling them
up as soon as the colour of the bloom shows and carefully
marking some of the best blues. Such care will be
amply repaid by the improved colouring of the strain.

There is a matter that is often overlooked in places
where garden gives place to woodland ; it is the character of the path itself. Where it passed among Rhododendrons and Azaleas it may well be of turf where these
are connected with the lawn. The mowing-machine will
clear the middle space, but it leaves a ragged fringe of
unmown grass on either side. The machine should be
followed closely by a man with a fag-hook or one of those
handy little grass-hooks that are in every catalogue of
garden sundries, so as to do away with the hard line left
by the cutting edges of the machine. The grass itself
had better not be of the brighter leaved lawn grasses
but rather of such as the fine-leaved Fescues of the wilder
uplands. But when the path gets into actual woodland
its character should alter completely. Here nothing
looks more incongruous than a well-made garden path,

perhaps even with a stone or planted edging. The woodland path should not be made at all, only cleared of obstructions such as invading roots or wide-reaching Brambles; something like a gamekeeper's path, only a little wider and clearer; the eye following it as an easy way to go without any visible making.

CHAPTER XXVII

THE ASIATIC PRIMULAS

THOUGH, with one or two exceptions, almost unknown to the ordinary gardener at the beginning of the present century, no race of plants has come to play a more important and valuable part in the furnishing of the modern woodland and water garden than the Asiatic Primulas. Thirty years of exploration and intensive horticultural discovery in China and its border-lands have added enormously to their ranks, while experience of the plants at home as they have found their way into gardens up and down the country has furnished ample proof of their high merits and sound garden qualities. The gradual extension of Primulas in cultivation and their prominence at various flower shows during the past few years should have resolved any doubts that may have been held regarding the place that the plants should have in all gardens, and if they have not yet received the recognition that is their due, it is no doubt partly because of the lack of the adventuresome spirit among some gardeners to experiment with new plants, and partly through lack of knowledge of the plants and their distinguished qualities that keeps them out of many gardens where they would find a comfortable and satis-fying home and contribute generously to the summer pageant.

On the whole they are an easy race, well mannered, of good temperament, and never troublesome to manage, either in the more ordered and disciplined places or in the more unconventional surroundings of the woodland or water-side where they are probably more at home, provided they have the conditions of soil and situation necessary to their well-being. Their cultivation, even to the beginner, presents no great difficulty, but it is as well at the outset to discriminate between the many different species, for they vary in their cultural requirements, in their constitution and their ability to settle down in new quarters. Such variation in behaviour is only natural and must be expected when it is remembered how wide is the geological distribution of the race and how varied the soils and situations where the wild plants are found growing. Some demand patience and care as well as special treatment to coax them to flourish, but the bulk of them are not difficult to please and will thrive under average garden conditions and with no more than ordinary attention. Nothing can be said against any of the species on the score of actual hardiness, for all are plants of the high hills, open meadows, and perfectly hardy, and any difficulties that have been experienced with some members in cultivation are due more to their dislike of the persistent wet of our average winter, the alternating periods of frost and thaw, and the lack of a definite break between our seasons.

For their successful growth the majority of the extra-European Primulas ask for nothing more than a moderately rich, well-drained loam, ample water during their growing season in late spring and summer, and an absence of excess moisture during the resting period in winter, and some degree of shade. The quality of the soil is always reflected in the appearance of the foliage of the plants, and in poor ground they will never have the same look of luxuriance, sturdy and robust growth that marks those plants that are grown on a more nourishing diet where the supply of moisture and shade is right. Excessive leaf growth, however, should never be aimed at, for large and coarse leaves, which are easily produced by some species, notably the vigorous *P. Florindæ*, when growing in a rich loam with plenty of moisture, are generally made at the expense of flower. Any ordinary garden loam enriched with a generous dressing of leaf soil and with the addition of gravel or sharp sand, if it is inclined to be heavy, will provide a comfortable root run for most of them, provided that it does not dry out too rapidly, and secondly that it is well drained, for there is nothing that the race, as a whole, abhor more than stagnant moisture. They do not flourish in light, sandy or clay soils, and share with Rhododendrons and Azaleas a dislike for limy and chalky ground, though in much less pronounced degree. In poor and thin dry soils it is useless to plant them without thorough preparation of the ground, which involves deep digging and the generous application of leaf-mould, fibrous loam, and possibly a little peat to supply additional humus, although the last is by no means necessary for success. For those who garden on chalk much the same advice applies.

All the Asiatic Primulas are grateful for some shade from the midday sun, but the amount they require depends almost entirely on the moisture supply and nature of the soil. In a rich loam with abundant moisture and no tendency to dry out the plants will stand and indeed appreciate more sun than if they were growing in a light soil that dries out rapidly. The main object of affording shade is to provide the plants with a cool root run, and, generally speaking, the gardener in the South will not go far wrong by giving them a cool situation where they are shaded from strong sun. In northern gardens, where the atmosphere is less dry, they can be trusted in more open spots, but always with some slight dappled shade. To grow them in dense shade is to court failure. On the one hand, they will not tolerate complete darkness and the drip of trees, and, on the other, they will not stand a sunny and dry place, and a situation where there is a happy mean between shade and moisture supply should be found for them. So much has been heard in recent years of the suitability of Primulas for water-side and bog planting that the beginner might be inclined to imagine that they will thrive in any waterlogged soil. With the exception of some of the more robust growers like *P. japonica*, *P. pulverulenta*, and *Florindæ*, and even these will resent such conditions in time, such is far from being the case. No Primulas will stand in a soil suffocated with stagnant moisture. They must have ample for their needs while they are growing, but equally moist conditions during the winter will result in a heavy casualty list due to the rotting of the crowns. Excessive wet during their resting period the majority will not tolerate, and the dislike is more obvious among the members of some of the many sections into which the race is divided, such as the *capitata* and *muscarioides* groups, of which the charming late-flowering *P. Mooreana* and the striking grenadier-like *P. Littoniana* are examples that have earned for themselves the unfortunate and unwarranted reputation of being biennial, as they die out in the winter after flowering, under such conditions. Good drainage is essential, particularly where the plants are growing by pond or stream and have plenty of moisture. If insufficient drainage is suspected in the subsoil it should be provided by removing some of the bottom soil and putting down a layer of broken clinkers some eighteen inches to two feet deep, and if the surface is heavy and sticky it should be lightened by the addition of gravel, ashes, or sharp sand to allow any excess of surface water to pass away freely. Nothing is more important to the general well-being and ultimate success of almost every member of the tribe than efficient drainage, and if the great majority of them have a well-drained, rich, and cool loamy soil that provides them with a fairly dry bed in winter there should be no risk of failure, and their best qualities will be revealed.

These cultural requirements, which after all are few, are nowhere better found than in the natural conditions of the wild garden and woodland and by the margins of streams and ponds, and it is for this reason chiefly that their use in such places is emphasised. It must not be imagined, however, that they will flourish in uncultivated places, in rank grass or rough herbage, and that they will thrive with all the vigour and luxuriance of healthy plants when they are given unsuitable positions and

*PRIMULA JAPONICA NATURALISED IN A MOIST
WOODLAND DITCH.*

EPILOBIUM TETRAGONUM IN COMPANY WITH FERNS LINING THE BANKS OF A WOODLAND

suffer from lack of attention.   Some of the more robust
species, it is true, are of such an enduring nature that
they will continue to grow for several seasons in a half-
hearted fashion, but there is a great difference between
sweeping drifts of plants that are perfectly comfortable
and those that are ill-nourished and wrongly placed,
and the gardener should see to it that the plants are
given good cultivated ground and proper and generous
treatment.

If the woodland and wild garden is well adapted for
their successful cultivation it is even more suited as a
background to the incomparable beauties of the race.
There is a seemliness about Primulas in woodland places
that is more readily felt, perhaps, than expressed, and in
company with such shrub aristocrats as the Rhododendrons and Azaleas they provide pictures of the most
enchanting loveliness.   Like many other plants, they
must be massed with a generous hand to be natural
looking and effective, arranged in bold masses to provide
broad sheets of colour, but always with an eye to affording the subtle and charming harmonies and striking
contrasts in colour tones that properly belong to any
piece of natural and pictorial gardening.   Nor is it only a
matter of colour.   Variation in form and texture of the
plant material is just as essential to the making of the
woodland or water-side picture where natural beauty
must always be dominant, and there is more than
enough to draw upon from the ample resources of this
handsome race to provide the most picturesque planting
incidents as varied in the delicacy or brilliancy of colouring as in the form and texture.   Few woodland effects

are more lovely than broad drifts of the impressive Candelabra Primulas, such as *P. japonica*, *P. pulverulenta*, or
P. Bulleyana, framed by bold masses of Rhododendrons
and Azaleas, which provide a setting of matchless beauty
when they are in their full tide of loveliness. But if
there is no piece of woodland available, then a planting
scheme on similar lines might well be carried out in any
cool and partially shady border where the plants would
be equally happy and comfortable.

In the same way most of the Primulas that are suited
to the conditions of the wild garden are admirable for
planting close to water by the edge of streams and ditches
and round the moist margins of ponds. There are few
gardens where a ditch does not exist somewhere on the
outskirts, even though there is no natural stream or pool.
Here lies an opportunity for the creation of a small
Primula garden. With comparatively little labour what
is probably at the moment a tangled mass of weeds and
a home of brambles and nettles can be transformed into
an attractive corner. In the cool soil of the banks and
along the bottom all the more vigorous species can be
trusted to flourish in the rough tillage and to naturalise
themselves when weeds are kept under, affording a picture of incomparable beauty and almost barbaric in the
splendour of its colouring in the early days of summer.
Here, as in the woodland, the beauty of the plants is
enhanced, without exception, if they are seen in the
mass, and if space is limited it is always better to restrict
the planting to one or two species, setting these with a
generous hand, than to grow small colonies of about a
dozen kinds of varying shades and differing in habit.

Colour value by the water-side, as it is elsewhere, is always strengthened by mass grouping rather than by planting small clumps which provide a restless and patchy effect.

Lack of knowledge of their ease of propagation is perhaps one of the reasons why many of the stronger species have been slow to find their way into the more unconventional parts of the garden. Almost all the Primulas that are good woodlanders and water-side dwellers are true perennials if the soil conditions, particularly in winter, are right. With one or two exceptions, such as the dainty and refined *P. Cockburniana*, they form numerous crowns from the one root-stock and consequently lend themselves to division, which can with advantage be practised every second or third year, or even every year in the case of some of the exceptionally strong growers or where a rapid increase of stock is desired. Frequent division is necessary if the flowering qualities are not to be impaired, for the greater the number of crowns, the less robust are the plants which have not sufficient room to develop properly, and the more weakly are the flower-stems and the smaller the flowers. There is no better time for the work, which is easily done by separating the individual crowns with finger and thumb, than the early autumn when the soil is moist and retains something of its summer warmth, and lifted, divided, and replanted about late August the young plants will soon establish themselves in new quarters. Failing early autumn the next best time is early spring when root action is beginning. One advantage of division as a method of increasing the stock is that it involves no extra space, and another and more important, especially with some of the species which vary enormously in colour when raised from seed, is that it ensures that the young plants are identical in flower colour as well as in other respects with the parental type. With *Primula japonica*, for example, which throws many different coloured forms in a batch of seedlings, the only method of obtaining a stock of a plant of good colour is by division.

Besides responding to division all the species, which concern the gardener for woodland and water-side planting, set seed with great abundance, and this if sown as soon as ripe germinates rapidly. The seedlings offer no difficulty and are easily raised in a moist and cool bed outside or in a cold frame which must be shaded from strong sunshine, in a light porous compost of loam, leaf-soil, and sand. Such species as *P. Bulleyana, sikkimensis, helodoxa, Florindæ, japonica, pulverulenta, Cockburniana*, and *microdonta* all respond particularly well to outdoor treatment, but it is essential to see that the seedlings never suffer from lack of moisture and that they are shaded from sun during their young stages. The only point that must be noted is that some species like *P. japonica* or *P. Beesiana*, and hybrid varieties such as the fine Red Hugh, do not come true to colour from seed, and with an especially good colour form of any of these variable types division must be resorted to as the only method of perpetuating a true stock. *Primula japonica* is an exceedingly variable species with flowers varying from white to rose and purplish-crimson, and as so often happens when the typical flower colour is red with a large proportion of blue in it, the majority of the

CANDELABRA PRIMULAS AT THE STREAM EDGE.

THE GRACEFUL PRIMULA SIKKIMENSIS FURNISHING THE MARGINS OF A POOL.

seedlings raised will be of a bad muddy magenta tone, and ruthless selection is necessary among such worthless progeny. *Primula Beesiana* is another example which is extremely variable and throws many colours if raised from seed, largely by reason of the fact that it crosses readily with other species, especially the fine orange *Bulleyana* where the two are grown close together; and it was extremely doubtful if a true stock of this species existed in any gardens until a fresh supply of seed was recently collected and sent home by the late George Forrest. Much the same is true of *P. pulverulenta*, which gives a wide range of shades, some good, many indifferent, and others distinctly bad, if raised from seed, but with this species much has been done to select and fix good colour forms, and thanks to the patient labours of Mr. G. H. Dalrymple of Bartley, gardeners have now at their disposal a fine pink-flowered strain of this desirable species which comes absolutely true to colour from seed, and has been secured by constant selection over a period of years. In the same way the gardener at home can practise constant selection with such species as *P. japonica, pulverulenta*, and the newer *microdonta* which also exhibits marked variation, and in time will obtain some most excellent forms which can be trusted to come true to colour from seed. As the different species spread in cultivation various hybrid forms appear as a result of crossing, and apart from the older varieties like Red Hugh, a hybrid between *P. Cockburniana* and *P. pulverulenta*, there are now hybrids between the yellow *P. Florindæ* and the purple *P. Waltoni* with flowers almost intermediate in shade between the parents. The race as a whole offers remarkable scope for the gardener who cares to indulge in hybridisation experiments, but indiscriminate crossing should rather be subordinated to careful and constant selection of the best plants, a method which is more likely to lead to the production of the best garden plants and enhance the value of many members of the race for decorative purposes.

By far the most important section of the family from the standpoint of garden decoration as well as by reason of their many other virtues, including hardiness and ease of propagation, are the handsome Candelabras, so called from their tall flower-stems which carry numerous whorls of stalked flowers at intervals up the stems. They are essentially plants for massing in the wild garden, and colonising in the woodland and by stream and pond, but they will flourish in among shrubs in any cool border so long as the soil is rich and does not get too dry in summer, though perhaps in such a situation they will not wax as fat as they will in the more congenial surroundings of the stream-edge. Of their number the vigorous deep orange-yellow *P. Bulleyana*, as well as the hybrid progeny in shades of salmon, pink, and orange ; the rich reddish-purple *P. burmanica*, which will thrive under more sunny conditions than most ; the graceful rich golden-yellow *P. helodoxa*, one of the best of all Primulas, but which is seldom happy away from moisture ; and its close ally, *P. Smithiana*, which to all intents and purposes is the same ; *P. Poissonii*, which in its best forms is almost a plum shade ; *P. japonica* and *P. pulverulenta* and its varieties and strains, are all worthy of a place. If less easy than its relatives, on account of its short-lived nature and the fact that it does not lend itself to division which necessitates its being treated as a biennial and raising a fresh stock from seed every year, *P. Cockburniana* is still worth bringing in to complete the roll of the Candelabras for the sake of its dainty habit and the rich orange of its flowers. It is a charming little plant, only about a foot high, well worth growing for its brilliance of colour which has gone to the making of that gorgeous hybrid Red Hugh, another and one of the most glorious members of the tribe that should on no account be omitted from any woodland or water-side scheme. Where it has been given up, however, the newer *P. chungensis* might well be tried, for if not so brilliant in shade it is less difficult to please.

Next in order of merit comes the group headed by the graceful soft yellow *P. sikkimensis*, which gives its name to the section. It is the *sikkimensis* group where refinement and elegance have been carried to a fine point, and happily they combine elegance and grace of habit with robustness of growth and good temperament. For the most part they flourish in the same situations that suit the Candelabras and have the same love for half-shade and moisture. *P. sikkimensis* itself is a most lovely plant, tall and graceful, with hanging clusters of fragrant, soft yellow bells, and it is never seen in better health than when it has its feet in ample moisture and some shade from strong sun. Though introduced a good few years ago, *P. secundiflora*, with drooping bells of a fine plum-purple set off by abundant white meal, has for some reason or other hardly yet come into its own. A species of excellent temper when it has a fairly rich soil and plenty of moisture, it is worth growing, and although it does not appear to seed freely it forms many crowns which are readily divided. In *P. rittata* it has a very close relative, much the same in its general characters and flower colour, and if the former is grown there is no need for the latter, which only differs in the upright character of the leaf rosette, unless there is room to spare. If *P. secundiflora* has been slow to find its way into general cultivation, the giant of the group, *P. Florindæ*, has had its merits quickly recognised. Though not yet of ten years' standing in our gardens it has come into the very front rank of garden plants. A most handsome species, robust, and perhaps even coarse rather than refined in its growth, with grand heart-shaped leaves which readily distinguish it from all others, and tall elegant stems carrying at their apices a loose cluster of some thirty bright sulphur-yellow flowers with a fragrance reminiscent of the common cowslip, it provides a magnificent effect in late summer planted in bold colonies by the water-edge. It is a plant of excellent behaviour, and though it is never seen in better and more vigorous health than when it has its feet right in the water, wedged between stones in the bed of a stream, it will grow wild and probably less coarsely in any cool and moist border in among shrubs. Less insistent in its demands for moisture than either *P. sikkimensis* or *P. Florindæ*, *P. microdonta* in any of its forms is another lovely and recently introduced member of the section that is proving perfectly at home in gardens, and will be comfortably placed in the coolness of a wood or in a north

AN EFFECTIVE PLANTING OF PRIMULAS SIKKIMENSIS AND MICRODONTA VIOLACEA
WITH MECONOPSIS WALLICHII IN WOODLAND.

THE STATELY PRIMULA LITTONIANA IN A WOODLAND CLEARING.

border. Almost reaching the size of *P. Florindæ* and with all the grace of *P. sikkimensis*, its hanging fragrant bells vary in shade from the pale sulphur-yellow of the variety *alpicola*, which faints to a creamy white in the charming form called Moonlight, to deep violet and plum-purple softened by a dense coating of white meal, the latter distinguished by the varietal name of *violacea*. There is perhaps no brilliance of effect about this species, one of the best of the recent new-comers to the race, but it is a plant of lovely charm and well worth a place in any Primula planting, for apart from its seemly grace and elegant beauty, its vigour and sound perennial habit are great points in its favour. To complete the section comes the port wine-coloured *P. Waltoni*, which, if less robust in nature, is nevertheless a species worth taking some pains with, for it has all the refinement and elegance of *microdonta*, associated with richer violet, almost ruby, colouring, dusted with a faint powdering of flour, and given much the same situation, it should prove happy and contented.

If these two groups provide the bulk of the best Primulas for generous planting in the woodland and by the water-side, there are many others in the genus which, if they demand more skill and patience and are scarcely so strikingly decorative in the mass, are none the less worthy of being accorded a place in some choice situation. The magnificent white *P. chionantha*, for example, is too good a plant to leave out of any stream-side planting. Though it belongs to a notoriously difficult group, called the nivalids, it has earned a reputation for good temper which is not unjustified, judging from its behaviour in many gardens. Given a rich soil, a moderate amount of shade with plenty of moisture during the growing season, and an absence of any excess in winter, it will flourish and make splendid clumps of handsome strap-shaped leaves from which rise the stout twelve-inch flower-stems carrying clusters of pure ivory-white flowers. In a situation it likes, especially one where it does not suffer from winter wet, it will prove fairly long lived, growing grander every year, but even where it succumbs to a trying winter climate it is worth the trouble of treating it as a biennial and raising a fresh stock from seed every year.

Also claiming a place in a shady border, a bed in woodland, or by the stream-edge is the striking *P. Littoniana*, one of the aristocrats of the family and easily distinguished by its elegant flower-spikes densely packed with deep violet flowers set off by bracts of brilliant scarlet that give it every appearance of a miniature Red-hot Poker. It is unfortunately only a biennial under our conditions, succumbing to winter wet after flowering, but, like *P. chionantha*, such a desirable plant merits the trouble involved in raising a fresh supply of plants every year from seed. It is never happier than when it has a rich porous soil, ample moisture while growing, and a position in half-shade. Suited for much the same situation is the lovely *P. nutans*, one of the most beautiful of all Primulas but confessedly one of the most exasperating, at least for those who garden under the more arid conditions of the South. In a cool and perfectly drained soil, rather on the peaty side so that it does not dry out in summer, it will respond by throwing

PRIMULA NUTANS IN A COOL AND SHADY BORDER.

PRIMULA ROSEA, A TREASURE FOR THE WATER AND BOG GARDEN.

up its mealy flower-stems, crowned by a short spike of almost cup-shaped bells of a lovely lavender blue. To see it in the coolness of a wood in Scotland or in the moist atmosphere of the West is to see it at its best with its flower-stems some fifteen inches high, but those who garden under less favourable conditions may be well content if its stems reach some six to nine inches high. Its recently introduced cousin *P. Wollastonii* is equally lovely, with tight rosettes of grey-green leaves densely coated with white meal on their undersides, from which rise six-inch stems topped by a tight head of deep, wide open bells of a rich violet-purple, softened by a coating of white meal. Much the same place as suits *P. nutans* should please this beauty from Nepal, but with its roots only just below the surface it is most insistent on a cool soil whose surface is never inclined to dry out. Both are plants of incomparable loveliness and well repay the care and trouble necessary to bring them to perfection.

The old *P. denticulata* on the other hand presents no trouble, and for all its rather coarse growth when compared to some of its relatives it is worth growing for its early flowers so generously given, its easy-growing nature, and the fact that it flourishes under drier and sunnier conditions than most. Its white variety *alba* is a plant of quality and beauty, and some of the improved and richer coloured forms introduced in the last few years are far to be preferred to the type. None need hesitate to grow it, for it is perfectly suited almost anywhere and everywhere, and in drier places away from the stream-edge its colonies should find a place, or in a border or even in the rock garden.

Though for some reason or other not so popular as some of its more recently introduced cousins, *P. involucrata*, one of the early introductions from the Himalayas, is too beautiful and too well-behaved and easy a Primrose to be left out of any water-garden. It luxuriates in a rich, moist soil, forming close-set tufts of dark green leaves from which rise six-inch stems topped with clusters of pure white, delicately fragrant flowers, and it never fails to flower generously every year, proving absolutely perennial in a situation it likes. Its close ally *P. rosea* also does well in the same position, and no one with a piece of moist ground at their disposal should be without this lovely gem. It is never happier than when planted in the wettest place, when it will grow into large and solid clumps of glossy leaves that smother themselves in loose heads of flowers of a rich pink carmine and need dividing almost every year, so vigorous is its growth in any open and boggy place. There are any number of forms, some larger than others and varying in freedom of flower and shade, but for the most part all are equally fine and can be trusted to give a good account of themselves with no trouble, provided they have ample moisture at their roots, when they can stand a fair amount of sunshine.

If less spectacular for woodland planting than some of the Candelabras, the fine *P. Mooreana* is none the less an easy and distinguished Primrose that merits a place in any collection, if only for the sake of its late flowering season. No objection can be urged against it on the score of beauty, however, for it is a lovely little Primula of refined colouring and habit, well worth planting in a cool border at the edge of shrubs or on the cool slopes of the rock garden, where its colonies will afford a fine carpet of deep lilac-blue throughout August. With its tight globular heads of lilac-blue flowers, which last in beauty for several weeks, rising on six-inch stems from close tufts of bright green leaves, it is a most attractive species and by far the finest member of the *capitata* section to which it belongs. It asks for nothing more than a well-drained soil, and though it will flourish in rich and moist ground it is more to be trusted in a place that is moderately dry, especially in winter, when it may prove longer lived than when winter conditions are against its survival.

To complete the list come two other fine woodlanders, both distinguished by rather handsome foliage, one unfortunately still scarce in cultivation, *P. heucherifolia*, the other a better-known Primrose called *P. Veitchii*. The former is an elegant and charming plant, more quaintly beautiful rather than showy, with its soft geranium-like leaves and graceful clusters of hanging tubular flowers of deep purplish-crimson carried on slender six-inch stems. It is never happy away from woodland shade and prefers a rich well-drained soil, and has an even stronger dislike of winter wet than most of the race ; and to make sure of a supply of plants seed should be sown every year. *P. Veitchii* on the other hand offers no difficulty in cultivation, and it is such a handsome species with its tufts of large-lobed leaves, from which rise the 9-12 inch stems carrying flowers of a rich reddish-purple with an orange eye, that it should be given a place in any woodland corner. It is not a plant that will appeal to those who like pure colours, but when grown in bold colonies in half-shade and in a cool and moderately light soil it is remarkably effective, and not to be neglected where there is room to spare.

INDEX